A.C.E.S. - Adult-Child Entitlement Syndrome

Barbara Jaurequi, MS, LMFT, MAC

authorHOUSE®

AuthorHouse™
1663 Liberty Drive
Bloomington, IN 47403
www.authorhouse.com
Phone: 1 (800) 839-8640

Published by AuthorHouse 11/16/2015

ISBN: 978-1-4772-8512-1 (sc)
ISBN: 978-1-4772-8511-4 (hc)
ISBN: 978-1-4772-8510-7 (e)

Library of Congress Control Number: 2012920424

Print information available on the last page.

Any people depicted in stock imagery provided by Thinkstock are models, and such images are being used for illustrative purposes only. Certain stock imagery © Thinkstock.

This book is printed on acid-free paper.

Because of the dynamic nature of the Internet, any web addresses or links contained in this book may have changed since publication and may no longer be valid. The views expressed in this work are solely those of the author and do not necessarily reflect the views of the publisher, and the publisher hereby disclaims any responsibility for them.

Acknowledgements

Thank you to:
Bill and Lois Wilson, Dr. Robert Smith and Rozanne S.
for the Roadmap. Special thanks to Joseph Dickson and
Tracy Holczer for teaching me how to follow it.
This book is dedicated to:
Diana Lozano – my best friend. Thanks for showing me the true
meaning of friendship. I don't know what I'd do without you!
Robert T. Nahas, James J. Nahas and Donna J. Barrack – my
"war buddies" and the three most awesome siblings in the
world! I love you guys. Thank you for the endless laughter
and for being there for me through thick and thin.
Albert P. Nahas and Rosemary A. Nahas – my father and
mother. Thank you for giving me my faith, my siblings,
and your love. I love you both so very much.
Nicole Michelle and Jamie Noelle – my two angels. You are magnificent
daughters and I treasure you both more than you could ever know - *at
least not until you are mothers yourselves!* Thank you for your sweet love.
I pray to be worthy of it as long as I live.
And to:
*Richard R. Jaurequi – my beloved husband who
happens to be the best man I've ever known.
I am blessed to "…trudge the road of happy destiny" with you by my side.
Our marriage is my joy and you are my happy place! I will love you
"…here, there, and everywhere" forever.*

And, above all, to:
**The Eternal Hero of all, *J.C.*, who placed all these
wonderful people in my life! Your love is amazing!!**

Foreword

As a licensed clinician in the mental health field for the better part of two decades, I have read many books focused on helping families develop healthy interpersonal relationships. What I've discovered is that most books written by mental health types are long on theory and short on treatment. In positive contrast to the glut of such publications is *A.C.E.S. – Adult-Child Entitlement Syndrome* by Barbara Jaurequi. Ms. Jaurequi has gifted us with a practical tool that is a clear and concise blueprint for families to actually change the way in which its members interact with one another, ultimately yielding the successful launching of their adult-children into the world of personal responsibility.

My personal experience counseling troubled parents and their adult-children motivates my high recommendation of *A.C.E.S. – Adult-Child Entitlement Syndrome*. I strongly encourage members of families afflicted with A.C.E.S. and all mental health professionals who work directly with families and couples to carefully study each chapter for the following reasons:

First, while *A.C.E.S.* is not a classified psychological disorder, this book addresses a growing phenomenon that is stunting the emotional maturation of many young adults, crippling their ability to become productive members of society and severely inhibiting older couples (or would-be *Empty-Nesters*) out of what should be a wonderful phase of marriage. While fraught with its own unique challenges, the *Empty-Nest* period should be a time when couples re-connect romantically after decades of active parenting with the ability to joyfully experience the satisfaction of successfully launching their adult off-spring into the realm of mature relationships and professional development.

Second, this book has been crafted in such a way as to be immediately practical. Part II of *A.C.E.S.* is fully dedicated to teaching how to restructure inter-familial relationships in healthy, satisfying, and meaningful ways. *A.C.E.S.* successfully conveys how to break the generational cycle of this devastating family dysfunction.

Third, while frustrated parents may initially be drawn to this book because of a desperate desire to help their adult-children take responsibility for their lives and to get them out of the house, these parents will find that diligent application of the principles, so effectively enumerated by Jaurequi, will also yield enriched marriages. They will find that true A.C.E.S. recovery results in greater self awareness, healthier boundaries, improved communication, increased personal accountability, and deeper emotional intimacy in their marriages than they ever imagined possible.

Fourth, to the best of my knowledge, Jaurequi is the only mental health professional to have the clinical experience, intellect, vision, initiative, and courage to put into writing what many families are experiencing in silence and despair. This book offers families afflicted with A.C.E.S. new hope for a brighter future.

In summary, *A.C.E.S. – Adult-Child Entitlement Syndrome* is a sorely needed resource for those families enduring a "failure to launch." It is a direct and practical work that eschews political correctness and "tells it like it is." I welcome Jaurequi's bold and valuable contribution to psychotherapy in the hope that her work stimulates additional dialog and research into what has, until now, been a neglected aspect of Family Systems Theory.

S. Scott Sutherland, MA, LPC
Co-Director
Soldier Life Center

President
Psychology of the Body, LLC

A.C.E.S. adult-children say things like:

"Why should I waste money paying rent on some crummy apartment when I can live here for free?"

"I can't afford to give my parents any money for rent."

"I don't have to be at work until noon. My parents shouldn't bug me about what time I get up in the morning."

"I can't pay for my own cell phone or car insurance. I don't make enough money for those things. Besides, it doesn't cost my parents very much to keep me on their plan/policy."

"Why should I clean their house? I shouldn't have to clean up after my parents."

(To parents) "There's nothing to eat in this house. When are you going to do the grocery shopping? Don't forget to get my Gatorade."

(To parents) "Can I have some money for gas?"

(To parents) "What's for dinner?"

(To parents) "I'm an adult…I shouldn't have a curfew…I can come in as late as I want."

(To parents) "Mom and Dad, please help me…I'll never drink and drive again but I need you to get me an attorney or I'm going to go to jail! This is my second DUI!! Do you want me to go to jail?"

"But I'm my mother's best friend…if I move out it will break her heart."

(To parents) "I have been looking for a job…there's nothing out there."

(To parents) "I quit my job today…my boss is such a jerk!"

(To parents) "I know I went to school to be a court reporter, but it's too boring. I want to do something else, I just don't know what yet."

(To parents) "My credit card is maxed out. Can you help me pay it down? I promise I will pay you back when I get a job."

"When my dad gets drunk, I'm the only one who can reason with him. If I move out my mother will have to deal with him by herself."

(To father) "Mom is mad because you didn't remember to pick up the dry cleaning like you said you would. You should apologize to her, Dad."

(To mother) "Dad didn't mean to hurt your feelings, Mom. He's just tired from the week. You shouldn't be so hard on him."

(To parents) "I don't have enough money to pay for my car registration right now. If you don't pay it for me, my car will be impounded and then I won't be able to even look for a job."

(To parents) "There's plenty of room here. Why should I move out?"

(To parents) "Don't nag me about my drinking – I'm an adult. I can drink if I want to."

(To parents) "I had to buy a present for my girlfriend's birthday so I can't pay you this month for my cell phone bill."

(To parents) "What is it to you if I play video games all day?"

(To parents) "If you loved me, you'd help me out. I'm trying as hard as I can to find a job. What am I supposed to do? I thought this was my home. I guess you want me to be homeless."

A.C.E.S. adult-children tend to:

- *Oversleep;*
- *Not clean up after themselves;*
- *Make excuses for their adolescent behaviors;*
- *Quit perfectly good jobs because they don't "like" them;*
- *Squander their money on frivolous items;*
- *Have babies out of wedlock;*
- *Cry or pout when they get "in trouble" with you;*
- *Use a lot of foul language and behave disrespectfully;*
- *Expect to be included in your private marital business;*
- *Interfere in your marital relationship;*
- *Steal;*
- *Renege on financial bargains;*
- *Get arrested;*
- *Develop addictions, mood disorders and anxiety problems;*
- *Drop out of educational/career training programs; and*
- *Maintain an attitude of entitlement.*

If you have observed any of the above in your adult-child, your family may be suffering from A.C.E.S. so **READ ON!!!**

A.C.E.S. – *Adult-Child Entitlement Syndrome*

INTRODUCTION

As a Licensed Marriage and Family Therapist, my primary responsibility is to help people work through relationship issues of all kinds. In my private practice I support a client population consisting of individuals, couples, families, and groups (which are made up of individuals working together to overcome shared issues). I help people who are struggling to manage emotional or psychological issues that are directly or indirectly affecting their relationships at home, with friends, or in their careers.

Individuals may seek counseling to help them manage psychological problems such as depression, anxiety, bereavement, stress, addictive disorders, angry outbursts, thought disorders, a wide range of adjustment disorders, and more. Couples and families usually present with issues such as communication problems, incidences of infidelity, adolescent behavioral problems, childhood disabilities that are affecting the family as a whole, grief and loss, financial incompatibility, sexual/intimacy problems, and blended family matters that often necessitate the need for counseling.

Over the last several years, however, I have become aware of yet *another* problem that occurs in modern families which, until now, has gone unnamed. I have treated over 100 such families, and many times the number of married couples, for a condition I have termed *A.C.E.S. - Adult-child Entitlement Syndrome.*

Usually, the spouses in a family with A.C.E.S will come in for routine marriage counseling, having only minimal awareness that their at-home adult-child (*adult-child* to be defined as anyone 24 or older) could be a principal factor in their marital disturbance. However, a simple review of the clinical symptoms of A.C.E.S. facilitates their understanding that they are experiencing an occurrence of A.C.E.S. in their family-system.

The A.C.E.S. recovery program addresses and remedies the *family* dilemma of A.C.E.S. The process of A.C.E.S. recovery, as outlined in this book, teaches miserable couples how to restructure their marriages into healthy, satisfying relationships. And they learn how to launch their adult-children into the world of personal responsibility once and for all.

As previously stated, while clients may initiate therapy to help manage symptoms of anxiety or depression, chronic interpersonal problems, or addictive disorders, I often discover that these clinical issues, at least in part, stem from A.C.E.S. To that end, it is likely that many other psychological and emotional disorders develop as a result of A.C.E.S. And these disorders frequently distract from the need to address A.C.E.S. directly.

In families with A.C.E.S., there is at least one able-bodied, under-productive adult-child living at home. In these families, adult-children maintain dependency upon their parents for housing, food, car expenses, other living expenses and even medical care. Many of these adult-children continue to live with their parents long past the college years, whether they attended college or not, subsisting as unemployed dependent adult-children. Many are chronically *under*-employed, working part-time jobs in order to have extra *spending money*. It is important to note that when A.C.E.S. is present most adult-children do not consider using the money they earn, or otherwise obtain, to pay their parents for their living expenses. Nor do A.C.E.S. parents consider requiring their adult-children to support themselves financially which is equally dysfunctional and disturbing.

As the A.C.E.S. dilemma continued to present itself in my work, I came to identify very specific symptom patterns in both the parents and their adult-children. The consistency of the aforementioned symptom patterns allowed me to recognize what I consider to be a full-blown syndrome, the root of which is two-fold. First, the adult-children maintain a fully entrenched sense of entitlement to be cared for by their parents, financially and otherwise, indefinitely. Secondly, the parents believe they are powerless to change the situation and are paralyzed by guilt and fear over what could happen to their adult-children if they were forced to take responsibility for their own welfare. In my experience, this syndrome is not exclusive to any particular cultural or socioeconomic population. I believe that Adult-child Entitlement Syndrome (A.C.E.S.) can be present in any family that shares certain characteristics.

This book fully outlines the characteristics exhibited by families grappling with A.C.E.S. It also delineates the formula for creating an occurrence of A.C.E.S. It details the impact of A.C.E.S. on the family as a whole and particularly, on the *marital-unit* of the family. If you are able to recognize the presence of A.C.E.S. in your own family, you are likely to suspect the case studies contained within this book are about you and your own adult-child! The symptom profile of A.C.E.S. is truly that consistent among families who share the disorder.

Part II is devoted to detailing the A.C.E.S. recovery program. It outlines the step-by-step process of launching your adult-child into the world to care for himself independently. Part II also addresses how to reorganize your family, renovate your marriage during the A.C.E.S. recovery process, and teaches you how to greatly reduce the potential for an A.C.E.S. relapse.

In order to ensure confidentiality of past and present clients, the names and identifiable characteristics of each case study have been changed or modified.

Table of Contents

Part I

Understanding the A.C.E.S. Family Dilemma

Chapter 1 – The Characteristics of the A.C.E.S. Family-system

Case Study #1 – Randy, Carrie and Evan

Randy and Carrie have been married for 30 years. They married when Carrie was 20 and Randy was 24. They have one son, Evan, who was born when Carrie was 23.

Carrie was living at home when she met Randy. The oldest of eight children, her responsibilities were numerous and strenuous. She describes her childhood as her "first motherhood", having been required to participate in the parenting of her younger brothers and sisters from the age of 10. When Randy came along, Carrie felt like Cinderella being rescued by Prince Charming! They married after one year of dating.

Carrie looked up to her husband who was a really hard worker. Randy provided a wonderful lifestyle for Carrie and their son, Evan. To show her appreciation, she did her best to make a beautiful home for Randy. But no matter what she did, it seemed like Carrie could never quite please Randy. He always seemed like he was missing something. He was distant and often aloof.

He travelled a lot and worked very long hours, leaving Carrie alone to care for their son most of the time.

Carrie enrolled Evan in karate when he was six years-old. From the very beginning, it was clear that Evan was gifted when it came to martial arts. Over the next several years, Carrie's part-time occupation was chauffeuring Evan to his many competitions and martial arts events. Some of the competitions were in other states but Carrie never missed a single one. Because of his travelling schedule, Randy was not able to attend most of Evan's martial arts activities. Although Randy expressed pride in his son's accomplishments, Evan never felt that his dad was interested in his life. He became very close to his mother and was proportionally distant from his father. Likewise, Carrie became enmeshed in her son's life and achievements and became emotionally estranged from Randy.

Carrie would occasionally talk to Randy about their obvious marital problems. While Randy did not deny that there were problems, he didn't take any action to repair them. He withdrew further and further over the course of the marriage, leaving Carrie lonely and emotionally dependent on Evan.

When Evan was 18, he got badly injured during a martial arts exercise. Even after healing from his injuries, he was no longer able to compete at the same level he had before the accident. He became depressed, as his success in the martial arts was a big part of his positive self-image. Evan felt he hadn't much to be proud of without martial arts. Although he was able to attend college after high school, he soon dropped out claiming that his back hurt too much to sit in those hard classroom chairs for hours at a time. After a year or two of "bumming around" as his parents called it, he got a job teaching karate at the local martial arts studio. He was paid $35 for each 90-minute class he taught but he only taught 12 – 14 classes a week. Evan's monthly gross income was approximately $1,600.00 - $1,700.00. He had a $400 car payment, a monthly car insurance payment, a cell phone bill, a credit card payment and other miscellaneous expenses. However, Evan didn't have housing expenses, food, or medical costs to worry about and yet he lived paycheck to paycheck. He never seemed to have enough money to pay for the things he needed. Believing that Evan truly could not afford to give them any money, Carrie and Randy never asked Evan for a dime. In fact, Carrie often gave Evan money for gas and other expenses when her son ran out of cash.

When Evan was 21, he got a promotion at the martial arts studio to the position of assistant manager. He was required to work 35 hours a week. Evan took to office work pretty well. He still enjoyed being around the studio but was glad to stop teaching. He liked dressing up for work and got a kick out of being the boss when the manager was out. As a newly salaried employee, his income increased substantially. Carrie and Randy were very proud of Evan when he got his promotion. They were hopeful Evan would now be able to support himself since he'd be making so much more money.

As it turned out, Carrie and Randy were very disappointed when Evan began spending all of the extra money he was earning. He traded in his used compact car for a much more expensive sports car, increasing his payment by hundreds of dollars a month. He bought unnecessary electronic gadgets, expensive clothing, sporting equipment and the like. Carrie and Randy became resentful that their son still didn't seem to have enough money to pay them for housing and food when it appeared he had plenty of money for whatever luxuries he wanted.

Evan knew that his mother was a soft touch where he was concerned. He played on her heart strings, crying "poor" every time she asked him for money to help with expenses. And on the occasions that Randy tried to confront Evan's irresponsible behavior, Carrie, instead of supporting her husband, openly defended their son, further straining their marital relationship.

Finally, Evan admitted to his parents that he had accumulated $27,000.00 in credit card debt. Carrie and Randy were horrified and baffled. They couldn't imagine what their son could have bought for that amount of money. Evan explained that a lot of it was just for clothes "and stuff" which was not untrue. But the "stuff" Evan bought included such things as $5,000 dollar watches, $300 dollar shoes, $1,000 dollar leather jackets, $800 dollar electronic gadgets, $1,200 dollar bicycles, and so on. Over time, these purchases added up to tens of thousands of dollars and Evan wasn't able to keep up with the credit card payments and his other monthly bills.

Not believing Evan could get out from under his debt on his own, Carrie and Randy decided they would pay off their son's credit cards. But before doing so they made a verbal agreement with Evan that he would have to pay them back at least $400/month. Evan was grateful to Carrie and Randy and made the first few payments. After that, however, Evan's excuses over why he couldn't pay his parents started all over again.

This was about the time that Carrie and Randy came to see me. They had been fighting incessantly over what to do about Evan. Neither one of them was able to stand up to their son; Randy because of his guilt over being gone for so much of Evan's life, and Carrie because she was afraid to lose Evan's emotional support if he became angry with her.

Randy, Carrie and Evan represented a classic case of a family with A.C.E.S. The marital relationship was in a shambles, Evan had become a *full-blown compulsive debtor and spender and he was completely dependent on his parents. Evan was fully triangulated in Carrie and Randy's marriage, and the family tension was palpable.*

The first identified treatment goal was to get Carrie and Randy communicating in a healthy way. After years and years of dysfunctional communication, it required a lot of work to get these two people to listen to one another. After that, we worked on establishing trust. Carrie and Randy needed to redefine their marital relationship and begin living up to that ideal. Carrie had to learn how to rely on Randy for emotional support and Randy had to make himself emotionally present and available in the marriage. In therapy Randy and Carrie learned intimacy building exercises and began to know one another in a new way. There was a lot of work that had to be done on the marriage before I could even introduce the couple to the concept of A.C.E.S. After recognizing the characteristics of the syndrome in their family, the spouses became willing to embark upon the A.C.E.S. family recovery process.

Once the spouses were on the same page, they were able to see the role they each played in the development of A.C.E.S. Evan was brought into the therapy sessions and, in addition to working through the A.C.E.S. recovery process with his parents, was asked to go to Debtors Anonymous (modeled after Alcoholics Anonymous). Exhausted from dealing with angry creditors and sick of being broke all the time, Evan readily agreed he needed to do something to get his life under control. He joined Debtors Anonymous and began attending 12-step meetings regularly.

Aided tremendously by the 12-step recovery program, Evan was able to stop his compulsive spending and began to pay down his debt to his parents while saving some money each month. Evan had to make many cost-cutting sacrifices in order to get out of debt, including trading in his expensive sports car for a used compact car which required a lot of humility. But thanks to Debtors Anonymous and one-to-one therapy, Evan was able to humbly take responsibility for his life. He stopped blaming everyone and everything for his troubles and finally began to experience happiness from within.

It took Evan 18 months before he was able to live on his own in an apartment, but he did it! He moved into a very small studio apartment in an old part of town, but it was his own. Evan felt proud of himself for the first time since being a martial arts phenom. He was independent, confident, on his way to becoming debt-free, and living like an adult at the age of 29.

Carrie and Randy continued in therapy even after Evan was launched from the family home. They needed to work through a lot of old pain in order to be close and feel secure with each other. But because they were committed to the process, the marriage eventually healed and they are a happy couple today.

Description of the A.C.E.S. Family
– a Verbal Family Portrait

Randy, Carrie and Evan are a perfect example of a family with A.C.E.S. The 'family' was born when Carrie and Randy got married and its dysfunction was apparent from the start. A.C.E.S. grows out of the marital relationship. If the marriage is not solid, the family is much more likely to develop the classic characteristics of A.C.E.S.

From the very beginning of Carrie and Randy's relationship, they failed to get to know one another on an intimate level. They recognized and liked each other's *external* qualities. Carrie saw Randy as a 'Rescuer" who could save her from her unhappy life at home. Randy saw Carrie as someone who could maintain a home for him so he could be free to pursue his career ambitions. Carrie and Randy are a case in point: if partners love each other primarily because of what one can do for the other on an *external* level, their marriage is bound to be a troubled one.

Healthy love exists when we love each other for internal qualities such as core character traits, aspects of spirituality, and meaningful pursuits we have in common. Dysfunctional marriages exist when partners love each other only for external factors such as good looks, money-making ability, social status, and the like. External factors do not provide adequate justification for life-long unions. And external factors are never the sources of real marital intimacy.

A.C.E.S. Family Characteristic #1 –
A Lack of Intimacy in the Marital-unit

Marital intimacy rarely exists to any significant degree within an A.C.E.S. family-unit. This was true with Carrie and Randy. Intimacy requires honesty about one's intentions, desires, insecurities, fears, etc. Carrie and Randy were able to admit in therapy that their reasons for getting married were largely external. At the time, they were probably too young and immature to be honest with themselves about the true reasons they were choosing to get married. Immaturity allows us to override common sense, letting us see what we want to see and not much more. When marital-partners see each other as a means to an end (e.g., a chance to move out of the house), they are able to block from their conscious awareness any glaring red flags that may direct them to end their relationship. To heed the warning of those red flags would be to abandon one's "solution" to any number of personal dilemmas.

One example of a personal dilemma might be the desire to have children while not having a husband on the horizon. As women age, many worry that if they wait around for Mr. Right, they could wind up too old to get pregnant by the time they get around to marriage. So they end up marrying the first guy that is ready and willing to start a family.

Some people simply marry for money. These are usually people who have not been materially successful on their own, or people who come from impoverished backgrounds. They see becoming affluent (even via marriage) as confirmation of their personal worth.

A lot of people marry in order to feel validated for being 'marry-able'. People with very low self-esteem tend to think they cannot afford to be choosy when it comes to picking a mate. They marry whoever is willing to marry them.

An extremely common reason people get married is simply because they desperately want to avoid the pain (and inconvenience) of breaking up. Many partners who fall into this category are capable of recognizing that they are incompatible before they marry. But because they dread the pain, upheaval, and the inconvenience of breaking up, they tend to put it off as long as possible. They figure, "We're never going to break up anyway so we might as well get married."

Some couples fence themselves in by owning property and pets together. Some may even have a child. Naturally, these circumstances further complicate and inhibit a break-up.

The Difference between Love and Intimacy

Generally, while partners may not have an intimate relationship from the start, and even when their primary reason for marrying is externally based, they usually do love each other – but it is most often an immature love relationship. The good news for couples with immature love relationships, however, is that even when love is immature, it is possible for intimacy to develop with effort on the part of both partners.

It is important to clarify the difference between intimacy and love as the two are often confused. They are not mutually inclusive. Intimacy and love do not necessarily co-exist. When we examine the difference between internal and external qualities, we learn that couples can love each other for lots of reasons that have nothing to do with intimacy. For example, you may love your husband for being a good provider. You may love your wife for bearing your children. You may love your husband because of all the years you've spent together. You may love your wife for the way she manages the household. You may love your husband because he is a really great lover. There are all kinds of external things that make us love each other. External love is real. It is not necessarily artificial simply because it is not mature, intimate love. But, as previously stated, intimacy only develops when we share ourselves on *internal* levels. Please note that partners may be able to *recognize* and *value* one another's internal qualities. However, if partners don't share their internal qualities with each other, they will never become truly intimate. For example, a husband may have a beautiful devotion to God and faith. His wife may truly admire her husband for his spiritual practices. But if the husband does not share this part of himself with his wife, he will miss out on the opportunity to experience genuine spiritual intimacy with the person he's chosen to share his life.

What is interesting is that we can love without intimacy, but we cannot have an intimate relationship without love. Intimacy is a component of love. It does not exist on its own.

Intimacy allows us to let another person into ourselves. Say the word 'intimacy'. If you break it down it sort of sounds like 'in-to-me'. The building blocks of marital intimacy include our private thoughts, our flaws and insecurities, our concerns and opinions, our dreams, our regrets, our personal faith, and the traumas or triumphs that have profoundly impacted our way of being in the world.

Sex is an expression of intimacy, but only between two people who love each other. Sex, in and of itself, is not an intimate activity. Ask a prostitute how intimate sex (in and of itself) is. He or she will tell you it is simply a bodily function, devoid of meaning, when love is not involved. A couple trapped in an A.C.E.S. family-system may have an active sex life, but without intimacy, it may feel like little more than physical gratification.

During the dating process, some partners are able to share at intimate levels. They grow closer and decide to marry. But particularly in the early years of marriage, couples need to maintain and continue to develop their intimate relationships. Solid, meaningful relationships help couples weather the inevitable pressures of married life such as managing two careers, maintaining a home, dealing with financial concerns, relating with in-laws, and *co*-parenting. These types of pressures can make or break a marriage. And they all have the potential to interfere with a couple's ability to have an intimate relationship.

When couples who lack marital intimacy have children, their children are often *triangulated* (*see Part I, Chapter 4*) into their relationships. Tension naturally builds in marriages that lack intimacy. However, children tend to camouflage tension between spouses. Partners can easily channel almost all of their daily love and energy reserves into their kids, leaving virtually none for each other.

Children seem to need an almost limitless amount of attention but most A.C.E.S. parents give their kids far more attention than they actually need to feel loved and secure. While it is perfectly natural and necessary for parents to nurture their children, A.C.E.S. marital-units tend to *over*-nurture. A.C.E.S. spouses save little emotional energy for each other and their marital relationships become strained.

To illustrate what I mean, visualize a leaf off an ordinary tree. When the leaf is properly hydrated, it is supple, able to bend. But when that same leaf is allowed to dry out, it crumbles with just the smallest amount of pressure. It becomes inflexible and needs to be left alone so it doesn't completely break apart. Likewise, if spouses don't 'hydrate' their marriage, their emotional needs will go unmet by one another, causing their relationship to dry out and become very fragile.

Parents in A.C.E.S. families tend to seek out their children to get their emotional needs met. Unwittingly, the spouses subsist in cooperative but unsatisfying marriages. With their children picking up the emotional slack in their relationships, marital intimacy continues to break down within the marital-units. Sadly, these ever-decreasing levels of intimacy can go unnoticed for years. Children in A.C.E.S. families could be seen as the 'glue' holding their parents together.

A.C.E.S. Family Characteristic #2 – Guilt

An orientation of guilt on the part of one or both parents is another classic characteristic of the A.C.E.S. family. Referring back to the case study at the beginning of this chapter, both Carrie and Randy parented Evan through an orientation of guilt. Carrie was guilty for leaning on

Evan for emotional support from the time he was a small boy. Even though Carrie was often aware that she was sharing too much with her young son, she relied on him to meet her emotional needs. Carrie also felt guilty that Randy was gone so much, believing she was somehow responsible for the fact that Evan had an absentee father. Having come from such a large family, and realizing how valuable having siblings can be, Carrie felt tremendous guilt over not giving Evan a brother or sister.

Randy felt guilty for missing so much of Evan's upbringing. While he was off pursuing his career to further his own goals, Evan was put on the back burner by Randy. He observed the close relationship his son had with his wife and recognized that he barely knew Evan. Randy was awkward when talking to Evan and of course Evan was able to sense his father's discomfort and likewise felt uncomfortable. Randy felt guilty for not teaching his son how to be a responsible young man. He blamed himself for Evan's apparent inability to take responsibility for himself.

The guilt felt by each parent led them to overcompensate for their faults by enabling Evan's irresponsible lifestyle through frequent, unearned indulgences.

A.C.E.S. Family Characteristic #3 – A Multi-Generational History of Dysfunctional Parenting

Individuals, like Carrie, who were raised in highly dysfunctional families, are predisposed to parent their own children in a dysfunctional way. Carrie was forced into a parental role as the oldest child of eight brothers and sisters and got little individual attention. Determined that her son would not experience a similar upbringing, she decided to have only one child and devoted herself to him entirely.

Carrie catered to Evan's every need, leaving him little opportunity to develop a sense of personal responsibility. Evan lacked appreciation for all he was given in the same way that most of us lack *appreciation* for oxygen. We take it for granted. It's always there so we don't tend to acknowledge it as a gift to be appreciated. Carrie's efforts to spare her child any challenges set him up to be perpetually immature and dependent. Evan, quite naturally, developed a sense of entitlement to be cared for indefinitely.

Carrie's behavior as a parent was driven by her fear of Evan developing the same kinds of resentments towards her as she felt towards her own parents. So when Randy tried to hold Evan to reasonable expectations,

Carrie defended Evan causing additional marital strife. Interestingly, Randy did not pressure Carrie into holding Evan accountable for his actions even though he knew it was wrong to enable bad behavior. Randy was too afraid that his son would see him as the "bad guy" and thusly went against his fatherly instincts to accommodate his own fears and insecurities.

Together, Carrie and Randy enabled Evan to grow into an irresponsible adult-child.

Few would argue that when children are given a reasonable amount of responsibility in childhood they tend to grow into responsible adults. In contrast, when children are required only to tend to their schoolwork and the extra-curricular activities that are *important to their parents*, they grow up feeling that they should never be expected to do anything 'extra'. And they typically don't.

Characteristic #4 – Parents Attempt to Live Out Their Personal Dreams Through Their Children

Parents who attempt to live vicariously through their children demonstrate another characteristic of the A.C.E.S. family. Let me give you an example using an A.C.E.S. father and son to illustrate this characteristic.

Karl is an A.C.E.S. father who was too short to be competitive in basketball as a young man. His dream was to play college basketball for a big university but at 6'1" tall, recruiters passed him by. Karl started playing basketball with his son, Max, when Max was just six years old. Even when Max was a very young child, Karl saw athletic potential in him. He encouraged Max to play all kinds of sports but it soon became apparent that Max had a particular talent for basketball.

Karl sacrificed most of his free time to coach his son and even excused Max from basic responsibilities such as studying, cleaning his room, obeying household rules, etc., as long as he did well in basketball. But it eventually became clear that Max was not particularly interested in playing basketball. He preferred more sedentary activities which frustrated Karl tremendously.

As Max got older it became more and more difficult for Karl to get him to play basketball. That's when Karl began to manipulate his son into playing by offering him rewards such as a new car or a later curfew if he performed well. Sensing it was wrong to bribe his son into doing something he didn't want to do, Karl couldn't help himself. Karl felt *so good* when Max had a good game! When Max scored a basket, it was as if Karl shot the ball himself. Karl got so much *personal* satisfaction out of Max's basketball ability that he was willing to do almost anything to get his son to keep playing.

Max was able to recognize how important it was to Karl for him to play basketball which gave Max a commanding advantage when it came to getting what he wanted from his father. Karl's desire to experience success in basketball (vicariously through Max) helped to develop an extremely inappropriate and unhealthy dynamic in his relationship with his son. In this particular scenario, the person with all the power in the relationship was Max. This was the reverse of how it should have been. Karl should have maintained the power in his relationship with his school-aged son. But because Karl allowed Max's success to be more important to him than it was to Max, Karl was forced to surrender all his power in the relationship he had with his son.

Max came to extort "rewards" from Karl as *he* saw fit. For instance, Max said, "I won't play basketball this year unless you buy me a car." Karl responded by saying "I can't afford to buy you a car this year, son." To which Max answered, "Then I guess I won't be playing basketball." The next day Karl went shopping for his son's new car.

Ironically, after successfully manipulating his father into buying him a car he didn't deserve, Max actually became more resistant to playing basketball. He developed deep feelings of resentment towards Karl. Max felt that Karl forced him to play basketball. He sensed that he was being used to fulfill his father's dreams and it created a feeling that his father was indebted to him because of it. When Max became an adult, it was time for him to collect his father's debt. He did this by never living up to his potential. He maintained a pervasive attitude of entitlement. He always expected to receive something for doing nothing.

Let's use Carrie *(see Case Study #1)* as another example of a parent who attempted to live vicariously through her child. Recall that Carrie's parents never gave her any individual attention as a child. There was no one pushing her to develop any talents she may have had. Her parents had seven other children to tend to so Carrie was deprived of the recognition, support and admiration she desired from her parents. So when her son Evan demonstrated talent in karate, Carrie spent nearly all her energy helping him succeed. She showered him with praise and encouragement, things she'd always longed for as a child. When he was a success in karate,

Evan vicariously fulfilled *Carrie's* desire to be seen and treated as valuable and special.

Characteristic #5 – An Unstable Sense-of-Self among Family Members

The problem with devoting so much attention to children for their triumphs and defeats, in addition to the fact that it comes at the expense of their not developing a sense of personal responsibility, is that they fail to develop a strong sense of who they are. They can only identify themselves by their successes or failures. In short, they come to measure their worth by their *perception* of their *parents'* perception of them. It is our character assets and liabilities that allow us to know who we are and to develop a strong sense-of-self. But when we are elevated or devalued by the central figures in our lives as a result of our performances, we cannot help but to identify ourselves accordingly.

Likewise, a parent who measures his own worth by his child's wins and losses also suffers from a poor sense-of-self. Some examples of these self-measurements may be, "I am a good mother if my child gets straight A's in school", "I am a bad mother if my child gets into fights at school", "I am a good mother if my child is a star on the swim team", "I am a bad mother if my daughter isn't asked to the prom."

A strong sense-of-self allows us to be confident and to make healthy decisions. When we know who we are, we are less prone to seeing ourselves through the eyes of others. We become more capable of resisting peer pressure. We don't sculpt ourselves into whoever we think we ought to be to satisfy others. When we maintain a strong sense-of-self we are able to recognize our flaws without condemning ourselves for them. We celebrate our accomplishments without becoming arrogant. We trust ourselves and, most importantly, we take responsibility for ourselves.

The case study in Chapter 1 illustrates Evan's identity crisis when he was no longer able to be a karate star. He became depressed and unmotivated. He only knew himself through the eyes of his mother and others who thought he was *amazing!* Once the applause stopped, so did Evan. Had Evan been validated for his discipline and determination as opposed to his trophies, he would have fared better emotionally after the accident.

Characteristic #6 – Dysfunctional Communication and Mixed Messages

Being unskilled in the art of communication is a very common liability when trying to have healthy relationships. Although we possess innate abilities to speak and hear, that does not mean we know how to parlay these capabilities into effective communication with others. Simply being able to speak does not mean one knows how to directly convey a clear message. Being able to hear does not mean that one knows how to actively listen.

In families with A.C.E.S., dysfunctional communication patterns make up the bulk of family interactions. We will fully explore some of the typical dysfunctional communication patterns A.C.E.S. families share in Chapter 2. In this section, however, we will focus only on one particularly damaging aspect of communication: the Mixed Message.

Mixed messaging is at the root of many communication problems in A.C.E.S. families. An example of mixed messaging in a family with A.C.E.S. is giving a child money and reward items in spite of his unacceptable behavior. This practice is very common and is usually facilitated by a guilty orientation on the part of the parents (*see Characteristic #2 in this chapter*). For example, a recovering alcoholic father may decide to give his 22 year-old daughter a new car to make up for the way he behaved before he got sober. Never mind the fact that the daughter crashed the car she already had because she was sending text messages while driving. Never mind the fact that she lives at home, pays no rent, does not go to school and only works part-time. While it is easy to sympathize with a daughter who was exposed to multiple drunken scenes (or worse) during her upbringing, it is not in her best interests for her father to give her a car and, in the next breath, tell her she has to grow up!

The following is an example of a mixed message sent in early childhood. A mother tells her daughter, age nine, to keep her room clean and to put her things away. She may say, "I'm not going to pick up after you…if you want to live in a messy room, that's fine with me." But when the child is gone at school, the mother cleans her daughter's room from top to bottom. When the daughter comes home from school the mother tells her, "I'm not going to clean your room anymore. This is the last time. Now keep it picked up!" Once the daughter applies simple arithmetic she will understand that all she needs to do to get her mother to clean her room is to tolerate her mother's admonishments from time to time: 1) I mess up my room; 2) Mom yells at me for keeping my room messy; 3) Mom cleans my room and then yells at me a little more. *Mixed message: I'm not going to clean up after you / I'm going to clean up after you.*

Let's fast-forward 20 years and look at a similar example of mixed messaging between the same mother and daughter. The mother, while handing her adult-daughter 60 dollars, says, "Honey, I can't keep giving you money for gas. You have got to get a job." The daughter says she is going to get a job but needs gas in her car to go job hunting. The mother agrees and feels that she has no choice other than to give her daughter the gas money. The following week, no job has been found because no job has been sought. However, the daughter is out of gas again. She goes to her mother for gas money and the cycle repeats – endlessly! *Mixed Message: I can't keep giving you gas money / I will keep giving you gas money.*

Let's look at one more example of a mixed message being sent by a father to his young son. The father may say, "You better bring up your grades next semester or you're going to face serious consequences." The next semester the son brings home a report card nearly identical to the previous one. Without enforcing a single consequence, the father then says, "Listen, Joey, I mean it…you need to bring up these grades. You're not going to get to do a lot of stuff you want to do if you don't do better next semester." The next semester roles around and, once again, Joey does not demonstrate that his grades have improved at all but his father assigns no meaningful consequence. *Mixed Message: You have to bring up your grades or you'll regret it / You won't regret not bringing up your grades.*

The father in the above example was never specific about what would happen if Joey failed to pull up his grades and he never followed through on his threats to enforce "consequences". The father said "…you're going to face serious consequences…" and "…you're not going to get to do stuff you want to do…" What on earth does that mean to a school-aged boy? Nothing! Had Joey's father said something like "I'm going to talk to your teacher every week for the next two months and if she doesn't tell me that you've improved by at least one letter grade in math and reading, you will not get to play soccer in April." By being specific, Joey would have a much clearer understanding of what would happen if he did not bring up his grades. If playing soccer was important to Joey, he may have been sufficiently motivated to work harder in school. However, if Joey still failed to improve his grades because he made no serious effort to do so, HE SHOULD NOT BE ALLOWED TO PLAY SOCCER – PERIOD! But in a family with A.C.E.S., Joey would probably get to play soccer in April without having earned it. And Joey would have learned a lot about how seriously he needs to take his father's threats! *Mixed message: You won't be able to play soccer if you don't improve your grades / You will be able to play soccer if you don't improve your grades.*

Children, including adult-children in A.C.E.S. families, do not automatically self-regulate. Children rely on their parents to enact rules and consequences so they can *learn* to regulate *themselves.* Immaturity naturally causes us to avoid unpleasant experiences even if (particularly if!) the unpleasant experiences are good for us (*have you ever postponed a necessary dentist appointment???*). Through rules and enforced consequences, however, parents can communicate the importance of self-regulation with their children and their children will eventually learn this critical feature of mature functioning. Please note that self-respect, a true sign of personal maturity, is a natural byproduct of self-regulation.

If parents fail to teach their children that behaviors lead to consequences, we send them the message that they can 'beat the system'. In childhood, the 'system' is our parents and their rules. If parents are consistent when giving out consequences (both positive and negative), children learn how to be consistent as well. They learn to make adjustments to their behaviors in order to get the results they desire. But when children figure out how to 'work the system', they assume the power in the parent/child relationship. This is both backwards and destructive to everyone concerned, including the family as a whole. We will discuss the need for A.C.E.S. family members to assume proper family roles in Chapter 2 of Part II.

Of more concern is that adult-children (who learned how to work the system in childhood) can easily learn to work the system in adulthood. These individuals often become fonts of information about welfare, unemployment insurance, low-income housing, and so forth. They lose their motivation and dignity in the face of a *system* designed to enable irresponsibility. This is not a commentary on government social programs that were created to help struggling people get back on their feet. I'm referring rather to a *family-system* that enables irresponsible living.

In Chapter 2 we will go over specific dysfunctional communication patterns that are characteristic of the A.C.E.S. family.

Chapter Summary

While in most instances the characteristics of families with A.C.E.S. are glaringly obvious, many families look for evidence to disprove that their family is suffering from the syndrome. They consciously seek to deny and discount the indicators of A.C.E.S. in their families in order to avoid the discomfort of facing the problem. They desperately attempt to identify 'exceptions to the rules' and twist their personal circumstances around to support their contentions that *their* families do *not* exhibit the characteristics of A.C.E.S. Unfortunately, when this is the case, families will find themselves locked in miserably dysfunctional patterns with no end in sight. However, if family members can maintain open minds, be willing to suspend blame, and be brutally honest on personal and interpersonal levels, they can and will recover from A.C.E.S.

Chapter 2 – Relationship Hazards that Lead to the Development of A.C.E.S.

Case Study #2 – Brady, Lori and Don

I met Brady, the adult-child in this case, when he was in a rehabilitation program for drug and alcohol abuse. His parents enrolled him in this program after Brady had been arrested for drunk driving. After interviewing his parents, Lori and Don, I learned that their primary reason for putting Brady in a rehab program was because they feared that their son could be facing jail time. Their goal was to prove to the court that Brady had faced his problem with drugs and alcohol and was actively seeking help. They were hoping that by doing this Brady would be shown leniency and not face jail time. Brady's parents paid for his treatment and very costly attorney fees.

When I interviewed Brady I learned that, like his parents, his (sole) reason for seeking treatment was to avoid going to jail. He expressed no real interest in actually quitting drugs and alcohol.

After talking to Brady for a little while, I was able to identify that he was very emotionally immature for his age. He was 26 years-old but was dressed like a teenager with baggy jeans belted at his pelvis, a torn T-shirt with a rock band logo on it, untied shoes, and a backwards baseball cap on his head. He spoke like a teenager and used slang that I'd only heard coming out of the mouths of the high school teens I'd worked with in recent months. He used exaggerated hand gestures to punctuate his feelings of frustration over being forced to come to rehab and he had a bit of trouble maintaining eye contact throughout the interview. It was obvious that he was uncomfortable.

Naturally, we spoke about his trouble with drugs and alcohol and made some realistic therapy goals that included eliminating the use of drugs and alcohol at least while he was in treatment. While he recognized that he ought to permanently quit using illegal substances, Brady was adamantly opposed to abstaining from alcohol once he had finished treatment stating, "Why should I give up drinking? All my friends party all the time. If I quit drinking, I'd have no friends." Despite Brady's refusal to abstain from alcohol for good, he attended the out-patient program faithfully and never missed a single day of treatment. Brady was discharged from the six-week program after "successfully" completing treatment. Perhaps most importantly to this family, Brady was also able to achieve the goal of avoiding jail time.

While Brady's substance abuse issues were the main focus of treatment in rehab, we spent a lot of time analyzing Brady's lifestyle. It was important for Brady to recognize the relationship between his way of life and his frequent use of alcohol and drugs. In order for him to make progress, Brady first needed to concede that he was not functioning as a responsible adult, as his social activities had not changed at all since high school. His largely unstructured day-to-day life was impairing his ability to mature.

In high school, Brady drank heavily at parties and dabbled in recreational drugs. He admitted that he was a poor student because he hated to study. He reported that he only graduated by the skin of his teeth, with a large chunk of his credits coming from P.E. classes rather than academic courses. It is important to note that I experienced Brady as having above average intelligence which led to my assumption that his under-achievement in school was unrelated to his intellectual capacity. My suspicion was that Brady's poor performance in school reflected a lack of motivation rather than a lack of intelligence.

Brady graduated from high school without much of a plan for his future. He enrolled at the local community college and signed up for four classes. By his own admission, Brady did not regard his college career as a serious occupation, it was just "…something to do." By the middle of the first semester, Brady was failing two of his classes and nearly failing the other two. He decided to withdraw from the two classes he was failing and in the remaining two classes wound up receiving a D and a C-.

It was at this time that his parents began encouraging their son to get a full-time job since it was clear to them that Brady was not taking school seriously. However, Brady insisted he simply was not used to the college system and would do better the next semester. So Brady's parents, wanting their son to go to college and do well, paid for a second semester of college and all related expenses including the use of a car and its maintenance. They even gave him weekly gas money for the car. To top it all off, as a 19 year-old young man, Brady was given money for lunch on the days he went to school!

Sadly, his second semester went no better than the first. Brady was demoralized and embarrassed but disguised his feelings with anger and defensiveness. His parents were frustrated and confused about what they should do with Brady.

Inaction on the part of Lori and Don set the stage for eight more years of Brady's irresponsible behavior. He continually failed to fulfill his promises to succeed at school or at a job. His parents continued to invest in Brady, both financially and emotionally, in the hope that their son would eventually move forward in life. Throughout this entire period, Brady lived at home, paid no rent or household expenses, had his own room, his own bathroom, cable-TV, Internet access, air-conditioning, food in the fridge, and the freedom to come and go as he pleased.

There is context for the way Brady was living.

Lori and Don met at the age of 20. They were married when they were both 22. They came from very similar backgrounds in terms of the emotional dynamics in their respective families. Both Lori and Don came from dysfunctional households in which intimate relationships were neither modeled nor existent. Don's parents barely spoke to one another and eventually divorced leaving Don, an only-child, feeling neglected and lonely.

Lori's childhood wasn't much better than Don's. In addition to going to school, Lori had to work in her family's trucking business from the age of 14. She managed accounts, scheduled drivers, and did the accounting. Her contributions to the family business were compulsory, not elective. Gratitude for all the work she did went unexpressed by her emotionally absent parents. However, they did compensate her financially with an allowance that she managed responsibly.

Despite being emotionally neglected by their parents, both Lori and Don developed into self-reliant, responsible adults. But they harbored enormous resentment towards their parents for their inattentiveness throughout their childhoods.

When Brady was born, Lori and Don became determined to provide a better life for their son than their parents had provided for them. From the time Brady was a toddler his parents were overly involved in every aspect of his life.

As he grew, Brady demonstrated impressive athletic ability. Wanting to ensure Brady's success in sports, Don coached all of Brady's teams and forced Brady to work on his athletic skills outside of scheduled team practices. When Brady's grades failed to meet the minimum requirement of a C average for participation in after-school sports, he was suspended from the soccer and lacrosse teams. Don, not believing his son could pull up his grades on his own, would "help" Brady with his homework by virtually doing it for his son in its entirety. Subsequently, Brady's grades went up and he was allowed back on the teams.

Brady's sense of entitlement grew as his parents continued to reward unacceptable behavior. With each poor report card, Lori and Don lowered their expectations for their son. Brady likewise lowered his expectations for himself. He came to believe that his only responsibility was to excel in sports. His room was always a sloppy mess, his grades were atrocious, and he was blatantly ungrateful for anything he received from his parents. It never occurred to him to get a part-time job because his parents gave him money for practically anything he wanted.

Before Brady was born Lori and Don's marriage could be described as highly cooperative but entirely superficial. As the marriage itself was not particularly fulfilling, they each sought personal gratification in their respective careers and were enormously motivated to achieve their professional goals. While they were not connected on an intimate level, Lori and Don did share the common goal of making as much money as they could before they had children. They were extremely disciplined in terms of saving and investing and by the time they were 30, they were ready to have children. One year later, Brady was born.

While Lori and Don loved each other to some degree, they had not worked to develop their relationship whatsoever in the years before Brady was born. They had been so focused on achieving their external goals that they unknowingly neglected their marriage. So when Brady came along, he took center stage in the family with both parents channeling their love and attention into him. Not wanting Brady to ever feel neglected, Lori and Don were determined to give their son whatever he needed including an excessive amount of attention

Over the years, Don became extremely preoccupied with Brady's success in sports. As Don's devotion to his son's interests increased, his emotional availability to his wife decreased. As Lori's frustration and loneliness increased, *she turned to Brady to meet her emotional needs. Over time, Brady became privy to the private details of his parents' marriage. He ultimately became a medium through which Lori and Don communicated.*

However, as Brady got into his 20s, it became apparent that he was not developing into a responsible adult. Unaware that their behaviors and choices facilitated Brady's immaturity, Lori and Don began to pressure him to do something with his life. Lori was not fully aware of her emotional dependency on Brady and Don was unaware of how much he depended on Brady to fulfill his own dreams. Neither one understood that Brady was triangulated in their marriage.

Lori and Don devoted themselves to "fixing" Brady. They made suggestions, offered counsel, facilitated job opportunities, and made empty threats that they would kick him out if he didn't get his act together. They finally resorted to begging Brady to 'step up' and tried to incentivize him with 'rewards' if he would just move forward in his life!

When Brady tired of his parents' nagging and wanted to get them off his back, he would mobilize and either find a job or enroll in some sort of training/ educational program (which his parents would finance). But inevitably, Brady would either lose or quit his job once it became difficult or inconvenient. Whatever money he earned at the various jobs he'd held over the years was spent on luxuries for himself. It never occurred to Brady to pay rent and his parents didn't expect it. Brady quit every training/educational program he enrolled in when it became "too difficult" or "boring."

This pattern continued until Brady was 26 years-old. When Lori and Don finally came to see me for marriage counseling, they both expressed that the marriage was an empty one. They were vaguely aware that Brady's problems were taking a toll on their marriage.

After teaching Lori and Don some basic communication techniques and validating their individual feelings, we were able to quickly identify A.C.E.S. as a core problem in their marriage. We began the A.C.E.S. recovery process and Brady reluctantly moved out within 18 months of his parents starting treatment.

During their last session, Lori and Don reported that Brady had been employed at the same full-time job for more than a year and a half. Before he moved out of his parents' home, Brady was hired to drive a van for a senior citizens community, taking the residents to doctor's appointments and on various errands. He was taking a couple of classes at the community college in the evenings with the goal of being accepted into the local Police Academy. He moved in with his cousin, age 34, who lived a nearby town. The cousins split all housing expenses and seem to have a good working relationship. Lori and Don reported that Brady visits them on a regular basis.

Lori and Don's marriage is greatly improved since beginning marital counseling, but after decades of relating to each other on a superficial level they still struggle with issues of intimacy. However, they are determined to make progress and have remained engaged in the counseling process in order to achieve their relationship goals. Overall, both Lori and Don report that they have begun to experience their marriage as satisfying and meaningful.

Warning: Relationship Hazards Ahead – Proceed with Caution

In Chapter 1 we looked at the characteristics of families that already meet criteria for A.C.E.S. This chapter goes over six relationship hazards that, when combined, may prime marital-units to develop A.C.E.S. in the families they create.

By and large, the partners that make up the marital-unit in an A.C.E.S. family are ill-prepared for the challenges of marriage. Chances are they already made some hazardous mistakes in their relationship even before they got married.

Most marital problems stem from core incompatibilities between the spouses. While no spouses are perfectly compatible, some incompatibilities can develop into relationship hazards. I have found the primary reason many partners avoid facing the truth about their genuine incompatibilities are their fears of breaking up. What these couples don't realize is that simply acknowledging their incompatibilities does not necessarily mean their relationships should end. On the contrary, by acknowledging the discordant aspects of their relationships before marrying, couples can identify ways to compromise or completely resolve the issues that could eventually lead to marital and family disturbances. If you are a spouse who avoided dealing with the incompatibilities in your relationship prior to marriage, there is a good chance that you and your spouse went on to develop a case of A.C.E.S. in your family.

I've worked with dozens of couples who actually had very strong awareness of their relationship incompatibilities prior to marriage. Partners may have shared openly with friends and family members the concerns they had about their future spouses. But, unfortunately, their awareness did not prompt action to directly resolve the problems in their relationships. For example, a partner may have complained to her friends about her fiancé's spending habits. But rather than addressing the issue with her fiancé (with a commitment to resolve the issue before marriage), she chose to simply avoid the temporary discomfort of arguing about the financial incompatibility in her relationship, wrongly assuming that everything would work out once she and her fiancé were married. The eventual consequence of her decision was substantial marital discord when it came to financial matters.

Imagine buying a car even though you suspected it was a lemon simply because you did not want to upset the salesman by backing out of the sale. To do such a thing would be crazy! But couples who create families with A.C.E.S. do that very thing when they avoid resolving problems in their relationships prior to getting married. Although the problem of A.C.E.S. is what eventually drives such married partners into counseling, their troubles began long before their families developed the syndrome.

Married life comes with a certain amount of inevitable challenges. When those challenges, including financial and career stressors, home ownership, in-laws, illnesses and most of all, childrearing, are combined with incompatibilities and unresolved problems, marriages tend to decompensate. Initially, spouses become spiritually estranged from each other (which we will discuss in Chapter 4) and 'down-shift' into relating to one another on less vulnerable levels. Next, spouses fail to meet each others' emotional needs. This leads to physical distance and dissatisfying or non-existent sexual relationships. In order to avoid all of this, couples need tools to manage relationship stressors in healthy ways. The goal is to prevent ordinary problems from festering into full-blown marriage destroyers.

There is an expression that says, "If you fail to plan, you plan to fail." This is advice that bodes well for people planning to marry. Marriages work best when they are not "played by ear". Couples need to work from common communication plans towards common goals. You may be thinking that this advice is coming too late for you if you've been married long enough to have adult-children! But it is not coming too late. The fact is that partners who have been together for decades can actually re-start their marriages whenever they choose to do so. And this time, they can do it right! If partners are willing to avoid the six following relationship hazards, their relationships can be built on healthier ground. You will learn how to do this in Chapter 3 of Part II (*Renovate Your Marriage during the A.C.E.S. Remission Process and Beyond*). But for now, let's focus on understanding the following six relationship hazards that led to the *development* of A.C.E.S.

Relationship Hazard #1 – Premarital Sex

To an overwhelming degree, I found that spouses in A.C.E.S. families engaged in premarital sex. Furthermore, the particular marital problems these couples had were awfully similar. The most glaring problem was that the partners in these marriages didn't seem to know one another very well at all. In many cases, their world views were different, their priorities were not aligned, and they had no idea what made each other tick. The spouses were disconnected from one another emotionally, spiritually, and oftentimes sexually by the time they came to therapy. Experiencing mutual feelings of sexual estrangement, most A.C.E.S. couples reported that they could not recall a time, since being married, that their sexual relationships had been truly satisfying.

Although, in the vast majority of cases, their sexual relationships were established long before they decided to marry, many of these couples stopped having sex altogether during the course of their marriages. Many spouses didn't necessarily view one another as sexual beings anymore. Usually, the partners co-existed but did not healthfully relate to each other sexually or otherwise.

Premarital sex, opposite from what most people may think, all but stops the 'get-to-know-you' process. When a marriage has been consummated via the sexual act, it is said to have reached a pinnacle of sorts. The word 'consummate' contains the word 'summa' which typically is combined with 'cum laude' and customarily refers to one having reached the *highest level* of academic achievement upon graduation from college. Once a student has graduated summa cum laude, he has demonstrated a level of mastery over a particular area of study. He's done! Finished! He doesn't have to study anymore! He's graduated!!! Hooray!!! It doesn't work that way with relationships.

The consummation of a relationship, via the sexual act, should not be seen as a finish line (as is a graduation). In relationships, if we feel we have 'graduated' by having sex before marriage, we may assume we know all there is to know about our partners. We somehow stop feeling the need to *pursue* one another.

Once partners stop trying to know one another on deep and meaningful levels, their relationships are likely to stagnate and may ultimately die. Healthy relationships require partners to continuously learn about each other, to discover one another through a myriad of life challenges and phases. Having sex too early in a relationship stymies the learning process and triggers faulty assumptions.

When two people love each other, they are capable of growing in closeness whether they are able to have sex or not. This truth is illustrated by partners who cannot be together sexually for one reason or another. Their devotion often intensifies. Their commitments are placed on higher planes and their relationships seem to become richer over time.

Partners who save sex for marriage may come to value each other in profound and precious ways because of their mutual respect for one another. Their joint decision to abstain from premarital sex may even foster trust in each other's integrity because of their mutual willingness to honor their commitment to sexual-abstinence before marriage. If a couple is able to honor their commitment regarding premarital sex, they can avoid the burdensome distraction of sex and are free to pursue closeness in non-sexual ways.

Understandably, sex is an enormous temptation for new couples in love. It seemingly offers reassurance of love and commitment. It is exciting and arouses intense feelings of passion. But *pre*marital sex is actually a liability that frequently breeds distrust because sex outside of marriage does not *demand* faithfulness. Premarital sex deprives us of the joyful responsibility we feel towards each other to be faithful once we are legally married. Worst of all, sex outside of marriage keeps us from treasuring the unique gift of our partner's sexuality because it wasn't even worth waiting for.

In order to avoid developing A.C.E.S. in the families we create, our pre-marital task is to grow together in three ways: emotionally, spiritually, and practically. We will be able to work through nearly all marital challenges if we can relate well on these three levels. Consider how much time spouses actually spend relating to each other sexually compared with the amount of time they spend relating in emotional, spiritual, and practical ways. It is critical that these three areas of relating be as fully developed as possible prior to marriage. If these aspects of a relationship are mature and fulfilling, there is a very good chance that the sexual aspect of the relationship will likewise be reflected.

In Chapter 3 of Part II, married couples will be taught how to abstain from sex until they have developed their relationships emotionally, spiritually and practically. Spouses will engage in genuine courtships which will *culminate* in the physical consummation of their relationships. They will come to understand sex as an *expression* of marital love and realize its deeper meaning in the confines of an intimate relationship between spouses.

Relationship Hazard #2 – Dysfunctional Communication

In Chapter 1 we recognized dysfunctional communication as a primary characteristic of an established A.C.E.S. family. It is also a major relationship hazard which usually reveals itself early in the dating process. But many partners tend not to recognize dysfunctional communication as a potential relationship killer down the line.

Spouses who do not know how to communicate effectively with one another will eventually settle into a lasting dysfunctional pattern of communication which becomes their *communication norm*. Their style of communication becomes a 'dance' of sorts that both partners know well. The dance never changes rhythm. In due course, it becomes too tiresome to engage in, causing the spouses to avoid necessary interactions.

Communication most often occurs between two parties. But sometimes third parties are involved such as media outlets which get information from one source and communicate it to an intended receiver. Sadly, third parties are oftentimes children in dysfunctional marriages, but we will wait to cover that unfortunate occurrence in Chapter 3. For now, we will focus our attention on dysfunctional communication in two-party relationships, specifically pre-marital/marital relationships.

Communication between two people requires that there be one Speaker and one Listener. For communication to be successful the Speaker must present his information clearly and the Listener must actively listen to that information and respond appropriately. This may sound like a simple mechanism, and one that is easy to master, but for many couples it is not.

Many Speakers make the common mistake of not being clear on their own messages. For example, a Speaker may be confused about what he truly wants to say and may not be able to find the words to convey what he is feeling. So if the Speaker is unclear himself, it is highly likely that his Listener will be as well. This is one of the ways misunderstandings occur and blossom into full blown arguments.

Sometimes, however, the Speaker may know what she truly wants to say but is trying to hide her true feelings for fear of being judged or discounted by the Listener. There is also a chance that the Speaker does not want to reveal her true feelings and is focusing rather on a secondary matter in order to merely express some of the emotion she is feeling.

Many times the Listener may fail to listen carefully. There is a chance that the Listener assumes he already knows what the other person is trying to say (i.e., he believes he's heard it all a million times before, etc.). It is possible that he may not be listening at all. Rather, he is simply waiting for the Speaker to finish talking so he can make his own point.

Some partners may leave an interaction feeling that they were misunderstood or that their motives were misinterpreted. They may feel that they were attacked unfairly. Perhaps the two parties became angry during the conversation and resorted to swearing. They may have even called each other names, which is one of the most destructive things two people can do in a relationship. Name-calling all but slaughters trust and intimacy between two people and usually only occurs when healthy communication has already completely broken down.

Some partners may keep secrets from each other which obviously inhibit their ability to communicate openly and honestly.

Time constraints could cause conversations to be terminated prematurely. The Speaker or the Listener could simply be poorly informed about a given topic and respond impetuously, effectively stymieing productive communication.

Couples who have grown weary after arguing about the same problems for many years may ultimately utilize the dreaded *Silent Treatment* as a way to communicate hurt or anger. Or partners may permanently keep their feelings to themselves in order to avoid angry, sad or disappointed reactions.

It certainly behooves spouses to learn some simple communication skills in order to resolve problems and to draw closer to one another. Some of these communication skills will be taught in Chapter 3 of Part II (*Renovate Your Marriage <u>during</u> the A.C.E.S. Remission Process and Beyond*).

Relationship Hazard #3 – Financial Incompatibility

In my experience, and in the experience of virtually all of my colleagues, financial incompatibility is one of the primary reasons couples seek marriage counseling. It is amazing how emotionally charged couples become when major or minor disagreements over money arise. Voices get raised, faces get red, defenses go up, eye contact stops, threats and accusations ensue and a hostile storm begins to brew.

Partners will oftentimes attempt to triangulate *me* into their relationship when it comes to issues concerning their finances. They appeal to me to validate their personal feelings. They make strong cases for their individual points of view, enlisting me as an arbiter of their disagreements. They look to me to render final judgments about what should be done to resolve particular issues.

While it is certainly tempting to take sides, I must resist the urge to do so. I must also resist the urge to identify solutions or compromises for couples concerning financial matters. I have learned that most couples are capable of identifying solutions that will work for them. My role is to address bigger issues including power struggles that punctuate most marital incompatibilities, including financial incompatibility. Spouses who struggle with financial incompatibility lack a spirit of cooperation with one another on money matters. They disagree about their financial goals. Some couples neglect their finances all together because they are sick of fighting about money. Shockingly, many A.C.E.S. spouses decide not to mingle their finances at all. They keep separate bank accounts and do not necessarily keep each other abreast of their incomes or expenditures. They say things like, "He pays the mortgage with his money and I take care of all the household bills with mine." They opt to exist as roommates sharing living expenses.

Before I got married, I lived with many different roommates. We shared living space. We shared in the responsibilities of keeping the common areas of the apartments clean. We split the costs of the utilities. We each paid our fair share of rent.

Oftentimes, my roommates and I had common friends and interests and we liked hanging out and doing fun activities together. In some cases, my roommates and I were not friends but we were cooperative with one another for the sake of convenience. If we weren't at least cooperative (i.e., downright unfriendly), the living arrangements would be dissolved as quickly as possible. It made sense to live with roommates at this time in my life. Situations weren't always ideal but, for the most part, living conditions were convenient, cost effective, and comfortable *enough*.

Some of my roommates became great friends, but none of them ever had access to my bank accounts. My roommates did not need to know what I was doing with my money. I didn't want to hear their opinions about my money management or lack thereof. I didn't want to hear their judgments about purchases I made. I didn't want them to expect me to lend or give them money because their perception was that I had an excess of funds. I didn't want to be put in positions where I'd be forced to trust them with the fruits of MY labor. It was nothing *personal* against them. It was just common sense. I needed to protect myself in case we had a falling out or such.

My experiences are probably fairly typical of what most people experience when living with roommates. And while these arrangements are entirely appropriate between roommates, they are utterly *inappropriate* between married people. Marriage is a special relationship that needs to be rooted in trust. If partners cannot trust each other with money, they certainly can't earnestly trust each other with far more precious matters including spirituality, sexuality, avocations, and most germane to the topic of this book, child-rearing.

When married partners come to me specifically because of financial incompatibility, I inevitably discover that their money problems represent only the tip of the iceberg in the overall condition of their marriage. Such couples characteristically have problems with communication, intimacy, sexuality...the whole gamut of relationship pitfalls. While financial incompatibility may seem like a minor issue in comparison to other relationship pitfalls, it is very often the first thing I suggest we address in therapy once the spouses have learned some basic communication skills. The reason for this is simple: *if married partners can work together to achieve a tangible goal, such as a financial goal, they will have more confidence when it comes to resolving other relationship problems.*

Money is a tangible entity. We can see it and touch it. We can even hear money when coins clink on a table. We can watch bank account balances go up and we can see them come down. We can measure debt and accumulate savings. We can pay off bills and we can (eventually) own our homes outright! We can invest and we can gamble with our money. We can lend it, gift it, spend it...my goodness, there are so many things we can do with money! But when spouses do not agree about what to do with their money, it can be disastrous for their marriages.

In families with A.C.E.S., the marital-unit is very often financially incompatible when they begin the counseling process. When we review how the matter of money was approached prior to marriage, the spouses usually admit they did not thoroughly discuss and resolve their differences when it came to finances. They may have had some idea about their partner's general attitude regarding money, but the topic was avoided because both partners believed their differences would be resolved once they were married.

Ask yourself the following questions: Did you recognize whether your spouse was a saver or a spender? Did you *fully accept* his or her proclivity to spend or save? Was he or she materialistic or thrifty? Did you accept his or her attitudes about money? Did he or she plan for the future or live only in the moment when it came to money? If you disagreed with your partner's attitude about money, did you think you could persuade him or her to eventually see things your way? If your partner brought debt or other financial obligations to the marriage (such as child support or alimony), did you undertake this reality without objections or hidden resentments? If you brought the debt, was your partner accepting or condemning of that fact? Did you discuss whether both partners would continue working after children were born?

After you have honestly answered these questions, you may have discovered that a lot of strife in your marriage is due to financial incompatibility. The good news is that married partners can usually learn how to become more financially compatible if they are motivated to do so. In Part II we will explore the things couples can do to overcome this relationship hazard.

Relationship Hazard #4 – Spiritual and Religious Differences

A lot of couples who went on to create families with A.C.E.S. glossed right over the topic of spirituality during their dating processes. Some couples may have addressed it after becoming engaged but quite often that was simply due to the need to arrange their wedding ceremonies.

Partners oftentimes make assumptions about how their future spouse *will* feel about spirituality and religion *after* they are married. They believe that the seriousness of their commitment to one another will inspire the development of spirituality in their marriage. Sadly, this is folly. In terms of spirituality and religion, what goes on in the dating process is almost certain to continue after the wedding.

Partners intending to marry may have strong and opposing opinions about incendiary religious issues such as abortion, euthanasia, homosexuality and gay marriage but they avoid discussing these differences because they don't want to cause an argument. This is a huge mistake because opposing views on these issues can permanently and negatively change the overall opinions spouses have about each other.

I have found that couples who went on to develop A.C.E.S. in the families they created did not thoroughly address the subjects of spirituality and religion prior to marriage but rather made *assumptions based on what they could easily observe.* For example, if a wife's husband went to church with her when they were dating, she might have assumed that religion was important to him when, in actuality, he was simply trying to please her because he knew religion was important to *her.*

It's very common for A.C.E.S. spouses to avoid discussions about how much time would be devoted to spirituality after marriage. Often one partner was intimidated by the topic of spirituality. He may have been fearful about being required to change his lifestyle if he agreed to adopt a spiritual practice or religion. One partner may have been eager to share religion with her spouse. Attempting to please his fiancé, one partner may have gone through the motions of spiritual and religious practices during the engagement only to stop this practice after getting married. Partners may have disagreed about how their children would be raised in terms of religion. One partner might have longed for spiritual intimacy while the other partner was made very uncomfortable by joint prayer and spiritual activities. One partner may have judged the other for being spiritually or morally inferior, thereby contributing to the development of a parent/child dynamic in their future marriage.

With couples who went on to create families with A.C.E.S., spiritual incompatibilities may have been extremely obvious in their relationships. But those couples believed that love could and would conquer their spiritual conflicts. Take it from a marriage counselor: spiritual incompatibility is as big a deal-breaker as any of the aforementioned relationship hazards identified in this chapter.

Since spirituality is perhaps the most personal aspect of our internal lives, we naturally want to be able to share it with our spouses. When spouses are not able to share this precious aspect of themselves with one another, they become lonely and estranged within their marriages. The void that is felt because of a lack of spiritual unity in marriages is troublesome in that the partners normally seek to fill that void independently, further alienating them from one another.

It is vital for engaged partners to address their spiritual differences prior to marriage in order to avoid this very powerful relationship hazard. If your family is suffering from A.C.E.S., chances are the partners in the marital-unit were spiritually incompatible from the start of their relationship.

Relationship Hazard #5 – Erroneous Assumptions

In families with A.C.E.S., it is almost a given that the marital-units fell prey to the fifth relationship hazard prior to marriage: erroneous assumptions.

Marriage is very serious business. Before entering into a life-long partnership with another human being, it is best to know as much as possible about that human being. We need to know how our partners think, what they believe, what they value, what they want, and what they are willing to do to make our marriages work. However, many people prefer to enter into marriage with blind faith that everything will work out despite the many dissimilarities between their partners and themselves across multiple areas. These people make erroneous assumptions about their partners in order to reconcile their decisions to go ahead and get married. They figure whatever differences they have with their partners can be worked out after they get married. They believe they will be able to change the point of view of their partners. They believe they will be able to persuade their partners to behave a certain way. They even think they will be able to change their spouses' value systems over time. These thoughts are wholly idealistic and utterly unrealistic. An individual who bases his decision to marry on idealistic and unrealistic assumptions is almost certain to experience crushing disillusionment about his spouse once his relationship becomes finalized through marriage.

The following are a few of the most common erroneous assumptions couples have presented in my practice:

1. Wife: I thought he'd want me to stay home with our kids…I never thought he'd prefer that I put them in day-care so I could work.
2. Husband: I thought she wanted a big family…but she's totally focused on her career. She says she only wants to have one child but not until her career is in place, whatever that means!

3. Wife: I thought he respected my career but since we got married all he does is belittle my profession and says I should try to earn more money than I currently make as an artist.

4. Husband: She was so affectionate and into sex before we got married...I thought she would be like that forever. Now she seems totally indifferent to having sex with me. Sometimes she even makes me feel like she's doing me a favor to have sex.

5. Wife: He played softball every Wednesday night before we got married. Once we had kids, I expected him to give that up so he could help me with the kids at night.

6. Husband: She had a great body when we got married...I thought she'd stay fit forever. But over the years she's gained a lot of weight and I'm not as attracted to her anymore.

7. Wife: He seemed comfortable with my family before we got married. Now he complains every time my family comes over. I assumed he'd want to spend the holidays with them.

8. Husband: I assumed she liked my friends when we were dating because she always seemed okay with me spending time with them. Now she thinks they are a bad influence on me and tells me she *never* liked them.

9. Wife: I knew he liked to drink and go to parties before we got married. But I assumed he'd be more responsible and mature after we got married.

10. Husband: I assumed she would always support my career since it provides the bulk of our livelihood. Now she acts like I "use" my career as an excuse to get out of being at home.

11. Wife: I thought he'd want to go to church with me once our kids were born.

12. Husband: Whenever I came over to her apartment when we were dating, it was neat as a pin. A lot of times she came over to my place and cleaned it all up for me just to be nice. I thought she liked keeping a clean house. But since we had kids, our place is a mess all the time. I hate it.

13. Wife: He acted like he liked to hang out with my best friend and her husband when we were dating. Now he tells me he

thinks my friend is a ditz and her husband is a bore. I assumed we'd get together with my friend and her husband on a regular basis but we hardly see them at all anymore.

14. Husband: She used to cook these gourmet meals for us – I thought she liked cooking and just assumed she would do all the cooking. Now she barely even goes to the market. We have frozen food most nights. I actually cook more often than she does.

15. Wife: I thought that once we had a family he'd be responsible with money. But he spends so much money on toys for himself. He is never satisfied and always wants the 'next greatest' thing. I have to be the money police and I'm sick of it.

16. Husband: I thought she would want to save for our retirement. It's just common sense. Instead, she accuses me of being "cheap" which really hurts my feelings. I'm just trying to take care of our future and she doesn't appreciate it at all.

17. Wife: I assumed he would support me when I wanted to get my master's degree. I always talked about getting an advanced degree and he never said a negative word about it. Now all he talks about is what it is going to cost.

18. Husband: She used to watch sports with me so I assumed she'd be okay with me watching football on Sundays. But now she complains every time I want to watch a game.

19. Wife: I assumed he liked going out on the weekends. We used to go dancing. We went to the movies, sporting events, concerts, all kinds of stuff. Now he says those things are a waste of money.

20. Wife: Since we got married, he's a total couch potato and never wants to do anything.

21. Husband: I assumed she would put some effort into her appearance after we got married because she always looked great when we dated. She used to dress really cute. Now she wears sweats and jeans all the time. She practically never puts on make-up anymore. And she wears these sloppy pajamas to bed. It's not very sexy.

34

22. Wife: He used to make a big deal about my birthday and Valentine's Day. I thought he was a romantic guy. Now, most years, I have to shop for my own present because he says he doesn't know what I want and doesn't want to get me the "wrong" thing.

23. Husband: I assumed my wife would show some appreciation for the fact that I have supported her and our family for decades. But she says I'm only doing what I'm supposed to do so why should she make a big deal about showing appreciation. When she says stuff like that, it makes me want to go into work tomorrow and quit my job.

24. Wife: I assumed my husband would pick up after himself and pitch in with the housework. When I ask him to do something, like vacuum, he will do it but he thinks he is doing *me* a favor. I work full time! But he seems to expect me to take care of the entire house, as if it is my sole responsibility. It drives me crazy.

25. Both: I assumed we were compatible because we got along great when we were dating.

I'm certain that troubled couples could identify many more erroneous assumptions in addition to the common ones I've listed above.

The bottom line is that if spouses want their family to recover from A.C.E.S., they will need to be honest about the expectations they had before marriage. They will have to talk about how they came to be disillusioned by one another. And finally, they will have to work through their differences, learn to compromise, and come to see one another in a realistic light through love, tolerance, and acceptance.

Relationship Hazard #6 – Difficult In-Laws

It is said that when we marry our spouse, we marry her entire family. So, in many cases, we end up getting far more than we bargained for once we've said "I do." When I meet with married couples for the first time, I try to get a clear picture of what their relationships were like before their marriages. In doing this, I am playing 'Detective', trying to find clues that would prove the couples' problems originated long ago, perhaps very early in their courtships.

When I ask them about their in-laws, partners very often will glance at one another as if to check whether it is a safe subject to discuss. Partners can become highly defensive when talking about their families of origin. I can usually tell right away if there is a history of in-law trouble in a couple's marriage simply by the way the partners react to questions about the topic.

If a problem with in-laws exists prior to marriage, there is no doubt about that problem persisting and worsening throughout a couple's relationship unless both partners are willing to recognize the problem from the beginning and take steps to avoid it escalating into a major relationship issue down the line.

For example, let's say throughout the dating process a partner's fiancé had to call her mother to "check in" every evening no matter what. If the daughter failed to phone her mother by a certain time, her mother would become worried, anxious, and angry and accuse her daughter of not caring about her. Rather than addressing her mother's anger and accusations directly and in an adult manner (e.g., respectfully setting limits and boundaries with her mother), the daughter would take the road of least resistance and just do what her mother wanted. While her fiancé may have voiced a strong objection to this *'Check-in-with-Mom'* arrangement, he didn't foresee the problem becoming worse over time and opted to not make a major issue of it prior to marriage. Had he anticipated his future mother-in-law's desire to be intimately involved in nearly every aspect of his marriage, perhaps he would have set a boundary with her and insisted upon solidarity on the issue within his marital-unit. But if this man went on to create a family with A.C.E.S., he probably expected he would be able to control his mother-in-law's behavior once he married her daughter. *(This is a good example of an erroneous assumption on the part of the man. See Relationship Hazard #5 in this chapter.)*

What this unsuspecting man does not understand is that his wife is legitimately handicapped by the emotional dependency she has on her mother. Not consciously desiring to be disloyal to him, the wife, during the marriage, would continue to prioritize her mother's desires above her husband's out of fear of her mother's reproach. This would result in a continuous battle between the husband and wife. The wife's mother would be triangulated into the couple's marriage. The wife would be in a perpetual state of conflict, torn between wanting to please her husband or her mother. In sum, the entire situation would become an enormous stressor for everyone. What a mess! If these spouses, *prior to marriage,* had been willing to deal with the issue of difficult (future) in-laws they might have been be able to avoid stepping right into this real relationship hazard.

Couples simply must address in-law problems directly and commit to resolving them *before* moving forward with marriage. The daughter in the above example would *need* to set a firm limit with her mother about the daily phone call business. Doing this could be very difficult without the complete support of her intended spouse. Take for granted that the mother was accustomed to being allowed to intrude upon the life of her daughter without reproach. So it would be a virtual inevitability for the mother to become angry and offended by her daughter's abrupt decision to change the way their relationship had always been. The mother would likely suspect that her daughter's fiancé was to blame for the change in the status quo which could set up a power struggle between the fiancé and the mother even before the marriage took place.

Trying to set even reasonable boundaries with the mother in this example would likely provoke anger, resentment, and jealousy which could last for the duration of the couple's relationship, or the mother's life, whichever came first.

Boundaries must be set with in-laws immediately after couples become serious about their relationships. In order for boundaries to be respected and honored, spouses must be in *absolute* agreement about the need to set boundaries with intrusive in-laws. They must be firm in enforcing appropriate boundaries.

If partners are uncertain or apprehensive about setting interpersonal boundaries with their in-laws, they should wait until they are on the same page (emotionally and practically) with their spouses before doing so. It goes without saying that setting limits with intrusive in-laws should be done in a respectful and loving manner. Both partners should be directly involved in drawing and enforcing boundaries with their in-laws impressing upon them that the spouses' loyalties lie with one another.

If couples want to avoid Relationship Hazard #6, they must understand the meaning of loyalty and its importance in a healthy marriage. When we marry, we make a commitment to forsake all others which includes extended family members, particularly if those extended family members are a threat to the stability of our marriages.

If your marriage has been riddled with problems that stem from poor in-law relations, you will need to restructure those relationships as quickly as possible. The first step in doing this is to recognize and admit the ways you have not been loyal to one another when you prioritized your family of origin over the family you made with your spouse. Remember to be patient with each other as you try to make amends for being disloyal over the years. It can be very painful to feel jealous of your husband's mother or your wife's dad because your spouse made his or her parent more important than you at times. You may have felt that you had to compete for your spouse's attention and affection which you bitterly resented. These are hard things to forgive quickly. It may take a considerable amount of time for these wounds to heal.

During the healing process, it may be helpful to keep in mind your spouse's actual intentions. In other words, it probably was not your spouse's desire to make you feel less important than her parents. It probably had more to do with her inability to set boundaries due to guilt and/or fear of her parents' reaction to those boundaries.

If you are a partner in a marriage that was compromised by problematic in-law relationships, you can testify first-hand that difficult in-laws are indeed a relationship hazard. The good news is that difficult in-law relationships can be managed and overcome if couples are willing to commit to the process of problem resolution.

We will revisit the subject of in-laws and how they can negatively impact a marriage in Part II, Chapter 3.

Chapter Summary

Indeed, it would be very difficult to find a married couple that didn't have *any* relationship hazards whatsoever when the partners decided to marry. No relationship is perfect. The point of this chapter is to highlight that couples, who go on to create families with A.C.E.S., often had multiple, easily identifiable relationship hazards prior to marriage that went ignored and unresolved, usually due to fear that they would be unable to resolve their incompatibilities without having to break up. Since breaking up was not something these couples were willing to consider, their problems worsened overtime and ultimately contributed to the development of A.C.E.S. in their families.

Wisdom tells us that the best way to deal with any problem is to first acknowledge that there *is* a problem. Clearly, the only path to resolution is a willingness to do the difficult work of fixing the problem. To hide one's head in the sand about obvious incompatibilities in his primary relationship is foolish. After all, no one can breathe with his head in the sand! Partners in marriages with multiple relationship hazards often report feelings of suffocation in their relationships. They tend to have the feeling that they are miserably trapped with one another. They don't understand how they could have become so completely incompatible during the years they've spent together when, in actuality, they were incompatible from the very beginning of their relationships. Hopefully this chapter has helped to clarify whether the differences between them were there all along and inspire them to resolve their issues at last.

Chapter 3 – A.C.E.S. Impact on the Family-system

Case Study #3 – Belinda, Rudy, James and Tony

James and Tony are the adult-sons of Belinda and Rudy who have been married for 37 years. They also have two grown daughters who married in their twenties and live with their husbands and children in nearby towns. But, prior to A.C.E.S. recovery, James (27) and Tony (29) still lived at home with Belinda and Rudy who became fed up with their sons' laziness and lack of ambition. However much they tried, Belinda and Rudy never seemed to be able to launch their sons into independent lives. They continuously allowed James and Tony to live at home for a meager $200 a month each. Both had their own rooms and lots of luxuries that they took for granted. Belinda and Rudy, then in their late 50s, both worked full- time.

Tony, having worked on and off for the last few years, collected unemployment which gave him enough money to pay $200 in rent to his parents, make his car payment, and pay his cell phone bill. The rest of his monthly income was spent on miscellaneous items such as gasoline and small personal necessities. He never had anything left over by the end of the month and had to rely on his parents when an unexpected expense (such as repairing his car) came up. When he still came up short, he explained to his parents that he simply did not have enough money to pay them his rent. Belinda and Rudy tolerated his excuses and Tony seemed to feel justified in skipping rent payments when he "…couldn't afford to pay" them.

Tony also relied on his girlfriend for financial "assistance". She worked full time, lived on her own, owned her car, paid all her own bills and was basically an independent woman. Why she chose to enable Tony's financial dependency upon her is the subject for another book!

Tony went to community college after high school and did fairly well but he dropped out in order to work for a construction company full-time. He was able to hold this position for 15 months until he was laid off "because of the economy." The sluggish economy was his excuse for sitting at home for several months at a time collecting unemployment until it ran out. This was Tony's pattern for many years, even when the economy was strong. He would work for a short while, lose his job somehow, collect unemployment, and then do practically nothing until he was forced to go back to work. He eventually fathered a child with his girlfriend but did not marry her and, until Belinda and Rudy decided to pursue A.C.E.S. recovery, never lived outside of their home.

James is just two years younger than Tony. Unfortunately, the two brothers have been somewhat jealous of each other their entire lives. If Belinda and Rudy gave Tony something, James immediately demanded he get something as well. The parents, terrified of being accused of showing preference to Tony, gave in to their younger son's immature demands. This practice set the course for Belinda and Rudy to go against their better judgment in order to please their spoiled sons. James did poorly in school and chose not to attend college after high school. During his freshman year of high school, he was tested for learning disabilities and was diagnosed with a reading disorder which made it difficult for him to retain information that he read. Belinda and Rudy used this diagnosis to lower their expectations for James. The truth is that James could have managed his mild learning disability had he been motivated to do so.

Belinda, more so than Rudy, never wanted James to be in a position in to fail because of his learning disability. Therefore, she defended James when he claimed that he wasn't able to study or perform well, even though he was enrolled in special classes that were designed to help students like James become successful. Rudy was able to recognize the fact that James was simply making excuses for his failings but Belinda fought her husband whenever Rudy tried to hold James to reasonable expectations. This caused a major schism in their marriage, exacerbating other problems in their relationship.

Belinda and Rudy met in grade school. They became high school sweethearts and married at the age of 21. Rudy had a drinking problem that caused Belinda to feel abandoned and neglected for the first 15 years of their marriage. Her resentment over Rudy's drinking throughout the first 15 years of their marriage was allowed to fester over the years and was never really worked through, despite the fact that Rudy had remained sober for the subsequent 17 years of their marriage. Belinda made it a practice to withhold sex for weeks or months at a time due to her anger. She relied on her sons for emotional support.

During their childhoods, both James and Tony had been witness to some horrible scenes as a result of Rudy's drinking. They had unprocessed resentment towards their father and most often sided with Belinda when she was upset with Rudy.

Eventually, Rudy had a series of extramarital affairs. Belinda became aware of two of the affairs and even separated from Rudy briefly, threatening divorce if he ever cheated on her again. Rudy asked Belinda to go to marriage counseling in order to work through their marital problems. Reluctantly, Belinda agreed to go to counseling but made it clear that she believed Rudy was solely responsible for the state of their marriage. Unfortunately, James and Tony were intimately aware of their parents' relationship problems.

After hearing their story, I suspected that the couple's relationship problems existed long before their children entered the picture. However, I was also convinced that A.C.E.S. was intensifying their marital misery.

Before I could introduce the A.C.E.S. recovery process, however, Belinda and Rudy needed to learn some basic communication skills. Their arguing was almost constant and they were in the habit of name-calling and using foul language when they became angry with one another. That needed to stop immediately in order for the spouses to demonstrate at least a modicum of respect for one another. Once the fighting was minimized we began studying A.C.E.S. and how it was impacting their marriage and the lives of their adult-sons.

Belinda felt judged and threatened when it became apparent to her that her sons needed to become independent men. It took a significant amount of one-to-one therapy for her to recognize how her sons had become triangulated into her relationship with Rudy. We addressed her fear of intimacy which stemmed from her traumatic childhood during which she was physically and emotionally abused by her parents. Belinda's ability to trust was all but destroyed as a result of her childhood and she came into her marriage in that condition.

Intimacy, a crucial aspect of a healthy marriage, is not possible without trust. Learning to trust Rudy, after all of his infidelity, was not an easy process. But by recognizing the part she played in creating her troubled marriage, Belinda's resentment towards Rudy was eased and she was able to begin the process of forgiveness.

Both sons were very resistant to the A.C.E.S. recovery process. A lot of work needed to be done in terms of family members assuming their proper roles in the family-unit (see Chapter 2, Part II). It made sense for James and Tony to move in together so they could share expenses but neither of them was willing to live with the other.

As sometimes happens, Belinda and Rudy had to force James and Tony to move out. Sadly, neither son believed his parents would actually follow through with the A.C.E.S. recovery process which required the brothers to be launched from the family home. They did not take advantage of the time they were given to prepare for the launch (13 months) and ended up leaning on friends and others to provide housing for them.

Tony tried moving in with his girlfriend but she eventually broke up with him when she was able to see how lazy he actually was. His sense of entitlement repulsed her. She eventually had to take him to court for child support.

James slept on friends' couches for weeks at a time until he'd wear out his welcome. For as long as he could, he 'couch-surfed', thereby inconveniencing anyone who was willing to oblige him for a time.

Once Tony and James recognized that they were not going to be rescued by their parents, in spite of their constant attempts at manipulating them into relinquishing their boundaries, the boys began to find their pride. In order to avoid homelessness, both sons miraculously got jobs that allowed them to live modest lifestyles. The sons somehow ended their life-long problems with each other and were able to find a one-bedroom apartment they could share.

Belinda and Rudy's marriage eventually improved with the help of marriage counseling and a willingness to relate to each other in healthy new ways. They have held on to their boundaries with their sons by supporting each other and focusing their energies on healing their marriage.

James and Tony have come to understand and recognize the presence of A.C.E.S. in their family and are no longer in denial about the dysfunctional ways they had been living. However, this family was **profoundly** affected by A.C.E.S. and has not fully recovered. Their resentments towards one another are deeply rooted. All are clear on the fact that it will take a considerable amount of time, as well as a commitment to the recovery process, for the family members to experience healthy relationships with one another. Fortunately, *each family member is willing to stick with the process until they make a full recovery.*

The Power of A.C.E.S. – Prepare for Impact

Now that we have reviewed the characteristics of an A.C.E.S. family and learned the causes of the family dilemma, it is time to address some of the ways in which A.C.E.S. impacts individual family members and families as a whole.

Once an adult-child has failed to launch himself from the family home within an appropriate time frame, his family begins to settle into a routine of sorts. The development of this routine is born of disappointment and is accompanied by apathy on the part of all family members. Over time, the routine becomes monotonous. The day-to-day rhythm in the home could be described as wearisome, boring, and dissatisfying for everyone.

While the family may be aware that the situation is not ideal, they initially resign themselves to the status quo. The family forms a kind of *co-op.* The adult-children and the partners in the marital-unit share space but live separate lives, coming and going with little accountability to one another. As time goes by, the marital-unit comes to view the adult-child as an "annoying housemate" who dominates the TV, eats all the food, and leaves dishes in the sink. Adult-children are particularly horrendous housemates in the sense that they don't even pay their fair share of household expenses!

With adult-children in the home, spouses suffer from a lack of privacy. They do not feel free to be a couple as they have not yet retired from the job of active parenting. Eventually, sexual intimacy within the marital-unit declines or does not exist in any consistent way.

One or both partners in A.C.E.S. marital-units often turn to excess food or alcohol as substitutes for a satisfying sex life. This behavior can lead to obesity or other health problems which might result in partners feeling less desirable and confident about initiating or engaging in sex. If the couple actually continues to have sex, it may become perfunctory and devoid of meaning. A lot of partners may simply become indifferent towards, or resistant to, having sex because they "are too tired." It is interesting to note that fatigue is a primary symptom of clinical depression which is frequently a symptom of the A.C.E.S. dilemma in some family members. Spouses, who become sexually estranged from one another as a result of A.C.E.S., may ultimately come to sleep in separate rooms which is a major intimacy blocker in marriages.

In their desire to escape the monotony at home, some marital-partners turn to the Internet to meet their social needs. Many spouses come to depend on Facebook, MySpace, LinkedIn, or virtual "life" games in order to relate to and interact with others. This business of socializing on the Internet, to the exclusion of socializing with one's spouse, is becoming a big problem in marriages today. Social networking sites facilitate the development of *preferred identities*. People routinely post altered pictures of themselves in order to project an image of their *ideal* self. Married people sometimes reconnect with past lovers which can lead to online romance and emotional infidelity. Dishonesty and secrecy abound in marriages where one or both partners misuse these sorts of Internet pastimes. In A.C.E.S. families, the desire to recreate oneself, albeit on the Internet, is overwhelmingly compelling considering the ease with which one can accomplish such a thing. A.C.E.S. family members can quickly become addicted to an unrealistic online world.

Sometimes marital-partners may neglect themselves physically. They don't make the effort they once did to be attractive to one another. They dress for comfort vs. style. The women may forego make-up. The men may skip shaving here and there. On the other hand, partners may become *hyper*-focused on appearance. One or both partners may have plastic surgery in order to be more attractive to the outside world which is more exciting and alluring than is the situation at home. Oftentimes this sudden change in attitude and behavior regarding appearance prompts suspicion which may or may not be unfounded. The partners, desperate for relationship satisfaction, may eventually engage in reckless behavior including extramarital affairs to mollify their needs.

Husbands or wives may be at the gym every day after work, coming home later and later in order to avoid the 'social' hour at home. Because it is morally acceptable and behaviorally admirable, exercise has become a common way to justify one's chronic absence from the home during 'family time' which for most families is during the hours after dinner and before retiring for the night.

Stopping off at a bar or restaurant bar with co-workers after work is also a common escape from the gloomy home-front for a lot of A.C.E.S. marital-partners. I have learned over many years as a marriage therapist that when alcohol consumption, loneliness, and opportunity collide, affairs are more likely to occur.

It's important to recognize just how powerful A.C.E.S.' impact can be on a marriage. If we consider that an extra-marital affair can actually be triggered by the problem of A.C.E.S., we must concede its potential to create considerable relationship trauma.

The impact of A.C.E.S. on adult-children is profound. The adult-child's immature behavior and attitude of entitlement usually reflects the severity of A.C.E.S.' impact upon him. While he may not demonstrate this feeling openly, the adult-child is likely to experience intense despair over the stagnation in his life. He may have fits and starts with school and various jobs but cannot achieve consistency in any one direction.

Parents may plead with their adult-child to get a full-time job or to pursue her education. Adult-children typically make lots of promises to fulfill their parents' requests but always have some reason they are not able to keep those promises. Adult-children are experts at describing minor barriers as insurmountable challenges to their parents. For example, an adult-child may claim that she can't go to school full-time because she wasn't able to enroll in the classes she needed at the community college because the classes were all full when she tried to register. Had this adult-child had the initiative, she could have registered for classes the minute registration opened which would have practically guaranteed her enrollment. But in a family with A.C.E.S., this adult-child would have blamed her failure on an easily overcome external circumstance.

As time continues to pass, an adult-child may come to see himself through the eyes of his parents who have begun to openly regard him as helpless and hopeless. The adult-child may internalize that he cannot complete anything and is likely to give up trying to reach goals.

If an adult-child earns money outside the home in a job of some sort, she will typically spend what little she has on small luxuries for herself such as electronic devices, clothes, expensive handbags and jewelry, cigarettes, mini-vacations, and the like. She may also spend money on minor personal expenses such as lunch out with friends or trips to the day-spa. Or she may simply blow all her money going to night clubs or buying drugs and alcohol. More concerning, in terms of an overall lack of ambition, is the adult-child who would rather collect welfare than look for a job.

After witnessing such behavior for a few years, parents in an A.C.E.S. family may become worried that their adult-child will never grow up. But at the same time they think it would be cruel to force their adult-child out into the world of personal responsibility because she has demonstrated she cannot take care of herself. She doesn't appear to have any meaningful goals. The parents are terrified their daughter will wind up on the streets if they kick her out.

A.C.E.S. parents, feeling both pity and shame over their adult-child's failure to launch, may actually enable him to continue living dependently. They may undermine his attempts to move out, yet be unaware that they are doing so. They do not realize that their son has become triangulated in their marriage (*Chapter 4 of Part I is devoted to the concept of triangulation in A.C.E.S. families*) and that their marriage has become emotionally dependent on his presence in the family home. Nevertheless, they may begin to see where they failed his as parents. However, despite the unhealthy and unhappy status quo, they are not able to concede this fact openly. Instead, they may look for outside reasons, such as the poor economy and the high cost of living, to justify their son's ongoing dependency.

In an attempt to give him a fresh start which might directly or indirectly facilitate his launch from the family home, many A.C.E.S. parents will offer their adult-child a substantial cash gift or loan. This money might be used to pay off enormous credit card bills. It could be used to finance a car. The money might even be used to pay for a stay at an expensive re-habilitation center/hospital if the adult-child is using drugs and alcohol. While A.C.E.S. parents may be well intentioned in their decision to give their adult-child large sums of unearned money, before doing so they would be wise to remember the following: 1) if the debt of an adult-child is paid off by his parents, the debt is almost certain to re-accrue over time. 2) If a car is bought for the adult-child, it is not likely to motivate a lifestyle change or inspire responsible behavior. 3) If a re-hab is paid for *(especially if re-hab was not the adult-child's idea)* it is sure to be a temporary fix. It is highly probable that the adult-child will resume use of drugs and alcohol as soon as he or she is out of trouble at home. My experience as a therapist tells me this. So does my common sense. Enabling irresponsible behavior is what gets adult-children into the A.C.E.S. predicament in the first place. Financing ongoing irresponsible behavior will only produce more of the same.

Usually, after many unsuccessful attempts to buy their adult-child some ambition and motivation, A.C.E.S. parents may finally stop giving their adult-children money all together (although they continue to provide food, housing, insurance, and so on). The sudden loss of unearned income may prompt adult-children to take drastic measures to get the money they need without having to fully support themselves on their own.

Shockingly adult-children such as these may actually prostitute themselves once their parents refuse to enable them financially. I'm not necessarily referring to sex-acts-for-cash-prostitution. Prostitution in the form of inappropriate relationships with "sugar daddies" or "cougars" who financially support adult-children in exchange for sex and companionship is the kind of prostitution to which I am referring.

Adult-children, who are no longer getting money from their parents, may otherwise engage in illegal activities such as selling drugs or shoplifting in order to get the things they want. If they wind up getting caught and are arrested, A.C.E.S. family parents are very likely to bail their adult-children out of jail and pay for attorneys to defend them in court. Despite the exorbitant cost of private attorney fees, adult-children see their parents as *responsible* for getting them legal assistance. Their sense of entitlement is so immense that even in the face of causing their parents to go into serious debt in order to bail them out of a self-imposed debacle, they rest knowing all will be taken care of by their mothers and fathers.

As briefly mentioned in the preceding paragraphs, alcohol and drug abuse are common problems among adult-children in A.C.E.S. families. Frequently, due to boredom and ongoing despair, adult-children may turn to substances to drown out the realities of life on life's terms. Consequently, they may be placed in *multiple* detox and rehab centers by their parents. Perhaps, even while having money problems of their own, A.C.E.S. parents often assume financial responsibility for chemical dependency treatment which can amount to tens of thousands of dollars over time. After years of living with a chemically addicted adult-child, A.C.E.S. parents are sure to be downright fed up! But, sadly, most of them believe their adult-children are utterly incapable of supporting themselves. They feel truly *trapped* by the circumstances.

A.C.E.S. parents may find themselves ashamed of their adult-child when talking about her to friends or extended family members. They make excuses for their adult-child or even invent plausible "reasons" their adult-child is still living at home in order to save face with those they feel will judge them as poor parents.

In a desperate attempt to get their adult-child moving forward, parents may pull strings or call in favors to obtain a job *for* her at a friend's company. The parents may even offer her a job if they own a business themselves. If and when their adult-child fails at the job, the parents are usually embarrassed but not surprised.

Many times A.C.E.S. spouses are at odds regarding what to do about their adult-child. One parent may say "enough is enough" and would be willing to kick his adult-child into the world to fend for himself. But the other parent might take sides against her spouse by vigorously defending her adult-child's *legitimate need* to stay in the home. This causes extreme strain in the marriage for the simple reason that one partner is prioritizing the welfare of another adult-person (the adult-child) over the welfare of her spouse. Make no mistake, if an adult-child is coming between the partners in the marital-unit of the A.C.E.S. family, the partners must recognize and remedy the situation or it will surely exacerbate anger, jealousy, and intense feelings of resentment between them.

As may already be apparent, A.C.E.S. family members effectively suffer from profound loneliness. Each family member experiences a pervasive sense of aloneness but does not necessarily express that feeling openly. All too often, and as referenced earlier in this chapter, this loneliness can trigger infidelity within the marital-unit. These affairs, emotional and/ or physical, are intensely damaging to the marital-system. Sometimes as damaging to marriages are platonic friends used to serve as emotional surrogates when partners no longer relate to one another on an intimate level.

With the goal of abating loneliness, adult-children may become sexually promiscuous, but cannot seem to form meaningful relationships. Conversely, adult-children may stay in long-term, highly dysfunctional relationships in order to avoid being alone.

A.C.E.S.' impact on families is far reaching and can even affect physical health. When family members experience deep-seeded anger that goes unexpressed, it can result in any number of physical ailments including headaches, stomach problems, and other chronic aches and pains. Obviously, if a person is suffering from any chronic health problem, regardless of its cause, he should consult his doctor or healthcare practitioner to decide on the best course of treatment for his particular condition.

Active A.C.E.S. also has the regrettable tendency to provoke compulsive, impulsive, and addictive behaviors in family members. A.C.E.S. family members often react to the general malaise within the household by forming addictive disorders which facilitate a temporary escape from unpleasant feelings. Practically speaking, any addiction that interferes with A.C.E.S. recovery (i.e. all addictions) should be addressed immediately. A.C.E.S. recovery is challenging even without the added stress of active addiction. It is extremely difficult for a family to battle active addiction and A.C.E.S. concurrently.

Finally, and perhaps the saddest impact A.C.E.S. has on families is complete spiritual collapse among family members. I define spiritual collapse as a condition that renders a person unable to see the meaning in most anything. Spiritual collapse causes people to become negative and destructive. Apathy flourishes. When experiencing spiritual collapse, people lack the joy that comes from having a sense of purpose. When we lose our sense of purpose, it is like a death of sorts. Lost purpose tests our capacity to defend the reason for our own existence.

It is so important that we not let a treatable problem like A.C.E.S. render our lives unhappy, dissatisfying and, worst of all, meaningless. On the contrary, we must face A.C.E.S. head on and trust that joy, satisfaction, meaning and purpose can and will be found in our family relationships once they are healthfully reestablished.

Chapter Summary

The impact of A.C.E.S. on any family is never positive. All family members become negatively affected by unchecked family dysfunction and sometimes the wreckage brought about by A.C.E.S. can be very difficult to overcome. That is why a specific program of recovery is necessary to rid your family of A.C.E.S. Fortunately, there exists such a program. You can look forward to learning all about it in Part II.

Chapter 4 – Triangulation and the A.C.E.S. Marital System

Case Study #4 – Tracy, Steve and J.T.

I first met Steve and Tracy when they brought in their 31 year-old son, J.T., for depression management. J.T. seemed resigned about coming to therapy. In fact, he seemed to have no anxiety about the process whatsoever. First therapy sessions usually involve an 'intake' in which the therapist gathers a detailed history of the client's life. For J.T. the intake seemed to be a rote and robotic process, as though he'd done it a million times before. As it turned out, J.T. had seen numerous doctors and therapists since he was a child.

Steve and Tracy had been married for 36 years and both described their marriage as comfortable, convenient, and economical. After only one session, I could easily see that the family members had very poor boundaries with one another. The parents spoke freely about their "loveless" marriage in front of their adult-son and it seemed that J.T. was fully aware and accepting of the state of his parents' relationship. No one seemed particularly upset about the situation. It was presented in an objective, unemotional way as though feelings of dissatisfaction were an irrelevancy.

Tracy and Steve rightly presented their son as depressed. J.T. certainly met the diagnostic criteria for depression. However, J.T. wasn't the only one in the family who was clinically depressed. Both Tracy and Steve appeared to be depressed as well.

J.T. reported feeling demoralized and overwhelmed by life. He realized that he wasn't growing as an individual but seemed clueless as to how to go about changing the situation. His parents were also in a quandary over what to do with their troubled son.

I learned that throughout J.T.'s lifetime his parents were hyper-focused on his achievements or lack thereof. They were overly concerned when J.T. began to struggle in math and reading. They started taking J.T. to doctors and psychologists when the boy was about eight years-old to find out what was "wrong" with their son. Eager to come up with a solution for Tracy and Steve, doctors and therapists were quick to diagnose J.T. with a variety of disorders including Attention Deficit Disorder (ADD), Dyslexia, Learning Disabilities in math and reading, and Generalized Anxiety Disorder. Some of the disorders identified by J.T.'s doctors were misdiagnoses, but ADD actually was a legitimate problem for him. In truth, ADD is often misdiagnosed and unnecessarily treated with prescription medication. But in J.T.'s case, ADD was a clinically justifiable diagnosis and a prescription treatment plan was indicated.

J.T.'s ADD could have been well-managed with the right medication and instruction in behavioral modification. But Tracy and Steve resisted medicating their son. Instead, they monitored his every move, thereby reinforcing the idea that J.T. was sick and needed constant help to function. Sadly, had J.T. been given the proper medication for his ADD, it might have made a big difference in his ability to be successful in school.

Focusing all of their attention on J.T., Tracy and Steve neglected their marriage. They rarely had sex and practically never went out without their son. Their conversations were typically about J.T. or some other practical matter.

In high school J.T. was placed in remedial classes in which he felt unchallenged. He referred to his courses as the "moron classes." Shame over his lack of success in school kept him fairly isolated. His socialization needs were met mainly by his parents. However, J.T., being a good swimmer, was able to maintain his place on his school's swim team which gave a bit of texture to his school schedule. Although he did not socialize with his teammates outside of swim team activities, J.T. got along with them pretty well. He also had great respect for his coach who was described by J.T. as supportive and motivating.

Outside of school and swim team activities, J.T. was home most of the time and his mother came to rely on him to meet her emotional needs, as her marital relationship had become boring and lifeless. One of the main problems in the marital relationship between Tracy and Steve was the lack of emotional intimacy between them. There was a mutual feeling of dissatisfaction with the marriage. While Tracy relied on J.T. to ease her emotional loneliness, Steve chose to cope with his feelings by over-working and socializing on the Internet.

Tracy routinely vented to J.T. about problems she was having at work. She also shared private information about her marriage including that she was no longer in love with J.T.'s father. Sometimes she would just complain to J.T. about her life in general. She would often thank him for listening to her troubles saying things like, "I'm so lucky to have you in my life to talk to..." J.T. felt a lot of love for his mother but he felt conflicted about being her friend and confidant.

J.T. felt anger towards his father for neglecting Tracy, assuming that his mother became reliant on him for emotional support because his father refused to meet his mother's needs. Bothered by Steve's preference to be on the computer instead of spending time with her and J.T. after dinner, Tracy became jealous of the social networking websites Steve frequented and resented that he had many opposite sex friends with whom he communicated on a regular basis. Tracy was unable to recognize that by using her son to satisfy her need for emotional intimacy, she was doing the very same thing she accused Steve of doing on the social networking sites. Understand that, in addition to people, individuals often rely on objects, behaviors, or substances to satisfy emotional needs and to diffuse tension in a dyad (two-person relationship).

After gathering a lot of information, I decided to meet with the entire family once every two weeks. I met with J.T. and the couple separately each week. I explained A.C.E.S. to the whole family and urged the family members to recognize the ways in which the syndrome pertained to their family. Once the three family members were able to agree that A.C.E.S. was at the root of J.T.'s depression and the couples' marital issues, they agreed to begin the A.C.E.S. recovery process.

After so many years of seeing doctors, therapists, and other specialists that were supposed to "fix" J.T., he struggled with the idea that he was capable of fixing himself. He truly did not think it would be possible for him to move out of his parents' house within a year. I recognized his anxiety about the changes he was embarking upon and tried to reassure him that he would have support throughout the A.C.E.S. recovery process. The healthy aspects of his support system would stay intact which included a couple of friends and his psychiatrist who managed his prescription treatment plan for his depression. His one-to-one therapy with me was also a core part of his support system. I also encouraged him to attend a support group for people with chronic mental illness which he was not yet willing to do.

As J.T.'s situation at home began to change, his depression symptoms became far easier to manage. His chronic low-energy and sleep disturbance (insomnia) began to subside.

Newly confident about his ability to take charge of his own life, and deeply resentful of his parents' tendency to try to control him, J.T. rejected his parents' suggestions vis-à-vis how to move forward in the A.C.E.S. recovery process. This troubled Tracy and Steve. They were afraid J.T. would not accomplish the things he needed to do without their guidance. But happily, J.T. realized on his own that he needed some counsel and decided to seek guidance from his old swimming coach who quickly became a trusted mentor.

J.T. applied for an Assistant Manager position at the coffee house where he'd worked part-time for eight months. He was offered the job which required him to work 35 hours a week. The subsequent increase in his income allowed him to move in with his coach's nephew who was in need of a roommate. J.T. signed up for an evening psychology class at the local community college as psychology was always a subject that interested him. Once he was on his own, J.T. seemed better able to negotiate former obstacles and to explore his options and his goals.

Unfortunately, Tracy and Steve's marriage was in really bad shape by the time we were able to address the way A.C.E.S. had impacted their relationship. It wasn't until they witnessed some positive changes in J.T. that they became willing to seriously work on their marriage.

Tracy had a hard time focusing on marital issues. She was preoccupied with sadness and fear about J.T.'s decision to move out. We decided she would see me individually for a few months while Steve saw a counselor of his own. After they had each made progress in individual therapy, the couple resumed marriage counseling and Tracy and Steve began relating to one another in a more appropriate way. They still have a long way to go, but Tracy and Steve recognize the positive changes they've made and in the relationship. Both are hopeful about eventually having the kind of marriage they both want.

What is Triangulation?

Triangulation is a psychological concept that was first introduced by family therapy theorist Murray Bowen in 1955. Along with another family therapy pioneer named Salvador Minuchin, Bowen was able to link the development of maladjustment in children to triangulation which, in simple terms, is a dysfunctional relationship device that is used to divert tension and conflict when two people are experiencing stress in their relationship. For triangulation to occur, a third person is drawn into the dyad (a two-person relationship) in order to diffuse relationship stress. Triangulation typically results in a *temporary* reduction of relationship tension though the essential problem remains unresolved. For our purposes, we will look at the triangulation process that goes on between the parents and adult-child in a family with A.C.E.S. Long before the adult-child becomes an adult, the marital-unit in an A.C.E.S. family has probably triangulated one or more of their children into their marriage. Bearing in mind that a lack of intimacy in the marital-unit is a primary characteristic of the A.C.E.S. family (*see Chapter 1, Part I*), partners may triangulate their child in order to satisfy unmet needs for intimacy and to diffuse stress and tension in their relationship. In a marriage where there is a significant intimacy deficiency, triangulation of the couple's children is almost inevitable.

Triangulation of a child can happen in more than one way. For example, in an effort to satisfy her need for intimacy, which is not being met by her husband, a mother may triangulate her child into the marriage by becoming excessively 'close' to that child. She may spend most of her free time with the child in order to eschew spending time with her husband. She may be hyper-involved at her child's school and in his extracurricular activities. Avoiding one-to-one time with her husband, she may refuse to leave her child with a babysitter on the grounds that she doesn't trust anyone to care for him properly. She may inappropriately confide in her child about the private details of her marriage. She may take sides against her husband in disciplinary matters in order to defend her child.

The woman in the above example seemingly demonstrates exceptional devotion to her child but it is obtrusive and unwarranted. The disproportionate amount of time she spends with her child impedes her ability to nurture her marriage. Her husband may enable the triangulation of his son and come to rely upon it, opting to let his son meet his wife's need for closeness. The husband may not be interested in trying to meet his wife's emotional needs himself.

Triangulation may also involve what is known as *scapegoating*. Scapegoating is a serious family dysfunction that involves one member of a family being identified as *the* problem in a given family. In unhealthy marriages, scapegoating of a child is quite common. Subconsciously responding to the tension in his parents' marriage, a child may act out in destructive ways in order to draw his parents' focus away from the marital stress. A child who is scapegoated commands a great deal of negative attention in a family and causes family members to spend much of their emotional energy 'fixing' him. Naturally, destructive behavior on the part of a child can wreak havoc on any marriage. But a child's behavior alone, even severely destructive behavior, is never solely responsible for major marital problems.

One example of behavior that could result in the scapegoating of a child is active addiction. An eating disorder, for instance, could create an enormous diversion from the pre-existing tension in an A.C.E.S. marital-unit. All the ups and downs that occur when dealing with the active addiction of a son or daughter could easily tear apart an already troubled marriage. Most often parents in an A.C.E.S. family do not agree on the approach they should take to help their child and this disparity becomes a further source of contention in their marriage. Disappointingly, rather than bringing the spouses together, destructive behavior on the part of the child usually only succeeds in causing ever more stress in the family as a whole.

Other examples of destructive behavior on the part of a scapegoated child may include drug abuse, chronic shoplifting, vandalism, cutting *(ritual and habitual superficial slicing of the epidermis)*, excessive piercing and tattooing, violence, academic problems, truancy, or any combination of the above. The bottom line is that if a child's destructive behaviors draw attention away from a troubled marriage, it will enable partners to avoid facing marital problems in order to focus on correcting their child's behavior.

On the topic of communication, triangulation causes exceptionally high levels of emotional reactivity between all members of a triad (a three-person relationship) making productive communication nearly impossible. Because each member of the triad feels unheard and discounted by the other two people, tempers flare as each person tries to communicate his point of view. Misunderstandings abound in triangulated relationships because a lot of what is communicated is done so second hand, usually through the triangulated member of the triad.

Due to the intense emotional reactivity within A.C.E.S. triads, spouses rely heavily on their adult-child to arbitrate their disagreements. Having become estranged in terms of their ability to communicate effectively, the spouses in an A.C.E.S. family (*as a result of triangulation*) communicate emotionally instead of rationally. They allow their feelings to overwhelm their thinking. As pertaining to the problem of A.C.E.S., spouses' ability to collaborate on important decisions concerning their adult-child is compromised. In sum, their dysfunctional interactions ultimately contribute to the development of A.C.E.S. (*see Chapter 2, Part I*).

Another troubling example of triangulation occurs when a parent and an adult-child align against the remaining parent. In an A.C.E.S. family where strained interactions are the norm, a parent/adult-child alliance can be disastrous for the marital-unit. As it relates to the development of A.C.E.S., problems within the marital-unit can cause the adult-child to feel obligated to remain in the home in order to prevent his parents from fighting or even from divorcing.

In a case where the adult-child feels as though he plays an integral part in his parents' relationship, he may be a willing intermediary in conflicts. He may suggest compromises, offer solutions, or even try to teach his parents how to get along by offering insights to one parent about the way the other parent feels. His goal is to restore the home to relative peace after conflicts occur. And his parents go along with this arrangement as they cannot seem to resolve issues on their own.

The following illustrates a typical expression of triangulation in a family with A.C.E.S.:

1. A conflict surfaces between two members of a family triad (in this example the conflict will be between the partners in the marital-unit).

2. The conflict escalates into a full-blown argument (i.e., explosion).

3. The family goes through a *decompression* period during which the members of the triad calm down. During this time the members of the triad deliberately avoid contact with one another in order to circumvent re-escalation of the conflict.

4. The uninvolved member of the conflict (the adult-child) is recruited by one of the parents. The adult-child is burdened with the knowledge of every private detail of the marital conflict.

5. The adult-child, desiring to restore peaceful co-existence between his parents, goes to his mother (or father, depending on the case) to help her understand his father's point of view. The mother, in turn, vents her frustrations about her husband to her son, further involving him in her marriage.

6. Once the decompression period has run its course, the family begins to communicate with each other about surface matters such as household business, etc.

7. Family members, relieved that the conflict is behind them, may begin to interact in a cooperative and friendly way.

8. The original conflict is never resolved because previous attempts have historically resulted in re-escalation of the problem. At this point the family returns to *homeostasis* which is a state of stability, dysfunctional or otherwise.

9. Soon, tension builds again which leads to another argument and the decompression cycle repeats.

With this sort of cycle repeating itself continuously, is it any wonder why the spouses in an A.C.E.S. family grow apart? Furthermore, is it any wonder why it is so difficult to launch a triangulated adult-child? The dependency the marital-unit has on its adult-child to maintain homeostasis is at least as problematic as the reliance the adult-child has on his parents to maintain his dependent lifestyle.

Chapter Summary

Without intervention, A.C.E.S. marital systems eventually become unable to exist exclusively on their own energy. The longer adult-children stay in the home, the more marital-units come to rely on them to diffuse tension in their marriages.

Going forward in your attempts to rid your family of triangulation, try to identify examples of triangulation in other areas of your life. You may be triangulated into a relationship at work with two of your co-workers. You may be triangulated in a relationship involving two of your siblings. Even your neighbors may communicate through you or you through them.

Consider whether you were triangulated in your parents' marriage. If so, it may seem *normal* to rely on your adult-children for what would otherwise be described as peer support. But seeking peer support from one's adult-child is not healthy; it is extremely damaging to inter-familial relationships.

In sum, triangulation represents a major barrier in a family's ability to overcome A.C.E.S. Family members need to rush to digest its potential to demolish relationships and seek to embrace the process of *de*-triangulation, a major aspect of the A.C.E.S. recovery program.

Chapter 5 – A.C.E.S. and Co-occurring Disorders

Case Study #5 – Skylar, Veronica, John and Patrick

Skylar was 28 years-old when I first began working with her family. Her parents, Veronica and Patrick, divorced after 17 years of marriage when Skylar was 10 years-old. Patrick was an active alcoholic when the couple divorced which enabled Veronica to get full custody of the children. Patrick was granted minimal visitation rights and only saw his children every other weekend.

As per the visitation agreement, every other weekend Skylar and her 14 year-old brother visited their father who lived in a small studio apartment. Severely addicted to alcohol, Patrick routinely passed out on the sofa while watching pornographic films even when his children were present.

For several months Skylar remained silent about her father's neglect and psychological abuse (exposing young children to pornography is rightly considered psychological abuse). Skylar finally confessed the truth to Veronica about what went on when she was with her father. Veronica was horrified.

Veronica refused to allow Patrick to see his children until he got help and had been sober for at least a year.

Shortly thereafter, Patrick went into rehab for alcoholism and achieved sobriety. He got rid of all the pornography in his home and cancelled all the cable stations that showed pornographic films. He also blocked access to pornographic websites through his at-home Internet service. He proved that he was able to stay sober and demonstrated that he was living a life of recovery. Eventually his court awarded visitation with his children resumed under much healthier conditions. Unfortunately, however, Patrick's relationships with his two children, particularly Skylar, were badly damaged.

When Skylar was 13, Veronica remarried. This time, instead of marrying an alcoholic, Veronica married an anger junkie. He was physically abusive from the very beginning of the two-year marriage. After being beaten, Veronica would run to Skylar's room. That's where she and her brother always hid whenever their step-father was having a violent outburst. Veronica would cry on Skylar's shoulder who would beg Veronica to get a divorce. Skylar was made fully aware of the emotional and physical abuse her mother was suffering and was used as Veronica's primary source of emotional support.

Finally, Veronica did get a divorce. She got some short-term counseling to deal with the trauma of being battered in her second marriage and four years later married a wonderful man, John, who was loving and supportive. John, Skylar's new step-dad did his best to parent Skylar who was a teen-ager when he and Veronica married. In therapy, Skylar expressed that she truly loved John and that he had always been a "great dad."

While the relationship chaos in Veronica's life ended when she divorced her second husband, her family was left with a multitude of associated problems that did not get addressed until many years later. The consequence of the many unresolved problems was A.C.E.S. and the development of various other psychological disorders as well.

Veronica's guilt over Skylar's upbringing was immense. She was able to recognize that her choices placed Skylar and her son in danger when they were children. Veronica understood that her children had suffered severe emotional and psychological trauma. The impact of that trauma was reflected in her children's behaviors and attitudes which were destructive and negative. Veronica had no idea how to help them. But rather than seeking professional help, Veronica tried to erase the pain of her children's childhood by showering them with love and indulgences. In other words, she spoiled them. She allowed them to miss school when they didn't feel like going. She bought them lavish gifts for no reason at all. She rarely said "no" to them and they had virtually no *responsibilities in the household. She gave them money even though they were old enough to hold part-time jobs. When they became old enough to drive, she bought them cars and gave them gas money.*

At the age of 22, Skylar's brother enlisted in the Navy and left home for good. That same year Skylar finished high school and found that she was confused about what to do with her life. She enrolled for classes at the community college with the intention of obtaining a certificate in early childhood education.

Skylar began to skip classes from the very beginning of her certificate program. Most often, she simply failed to wake up on time to go to class. Veronica and John began to feel frustrated. Veronica could not understand why her daughter was so unmotivated, particularly when she and John made it so easy for Skylar to succeed in school. Veronica believed that all Skylar had to worry about was attending her classes and completing her assignments. Skylar certainly wasn't burdened with financial obligations and didn't even have a part-time job to distract her from her studies.

Veronica began to resent Skylar for taking advantage of her generosity. She often told Skylar that she was a spoiled brat. Veronica felt that Skylar was taking everything she had for granted. According to Veronica, Skylar seemed to have no appreciation for, or awareness of, the financial sacrifices Veronica and John had to make in order to give Skylar the kind of lifestyle to which she'd become accustomed.

When her mother refused to give her anymore 'spending' money, Skylar got a job at a juice bar making smoothies and running the cash register. She was earning minimum wage and only worked about 15 hours a week. The rest of the time she hung out with friends and lounged around the house. After several months, Skylar quit her job explaining to her parents that it "...wasn't worth it...as soon as I fill up my gas tank, my whole check is gone."

Veronica and John continued to support Skylar well into her 20s. Five years after graduating from high school, Skylar showed little motivation to either obtain a degree or get a full-time job.

When Skylar was 23 years-old she became involved with a guy who used and sold drugs. His drug of choice was Oxytocin, a powerful prescription narcotic. Skylar sampled 'Oxy' and found that she loved it! She quickly became addicted and began using whatever money she had to buy the pills. Eventually, she began selling the pills in exchange for her own supply.

Veronica and John became aware of Skylar's drug use as her behavior began to change. Skylar was sleeping more than ever and seemed to have no interest in anything other than hanging out with her drug-using boyfriend. She became angry and defensive whenever Veronica "nagged" her to do something with her life.

John was openly frustrated with both Veronica and Skylar, but mostly with Veronica. He felt that Veronica held him back when he tried to set limits with Skylar. John recognized that Veronica's guilt over Skylar's childhood kept her from holding her daughter accountable for her reckless behavior. He watched his wife bail Skylar out of every problem she made for herself, despite John's strong objections. Naturally, over time, Veronica's enabling of Skylar came between her and her husband. The spouses became estranged sexually and emotionally.

Once again, as in Skylar's childhood, Veronica began to lean on Skylar for emotional support. Skylar was used to transmit messages between her mom and step-dad when the spouses refused to speak to one another for days at a time. Occasionally, during times of extreme frustration with Skylar, Veronica blamed her daughter for her marital problems: "If you would just get a job and move out of here, my marriage would get back on track."

Desperate to get her mom to stop nagging her about getting a job, and also desperate to have enough money to support her drug habit, Skylar began dancing nude at a club in a nearby town. Although she hated doing it, Skylar rationalized that she was making a lot of money without much effort. Unfortunately, the more she danced nude, the more she wanted the drugs to help her escape the guilt and shame over what she was doing to earn money.

One night, John followed Skylar to see where she was going as he had suspected Skylar was selling drugs to make all the money she suddenly seemed to have. When he discovered his step-daughter was dancing nude he insisted she quit, promising that he would help her find a decent job.

John followed through on his promise to find a job for Skylar. She was hired as a clerical worker in his friend's construction business. But unfortunately, Skylar was fired when she failed to show up for her very first day of work. This was about the time that Veronica and John first came to see me.

Veronica and John were miserable. Both were extremely angry and frustrated with Skylar. However, Veronica was also struggling with a powerful internal conflict between wanting Skylar to move out and her own guilt over the role she played in "...the way Skylar turned out." The internal conflict Veronica was experiencing was coming between her and John and their marriage was suffering as a result. John was openly considering separation.

Once Veronica and John were able to recognize how their family fit the A.C.E.S. symptom profile, they began applying the step-by-step process of recovery. Over time, their marriage improved. Veronica and John worked *towards restoring trust in one another which led to their willingness to de-triangulate from Skylar. As the A.C.E.S. recovery process requires, Skylar was ultimately launched into the world of personal responsibility to care for herself. But it wasn't a smooth transition for her.*

Skylar was highly resistant to the A.C.E.S. recovery process. She failed to take advantage of the 12-month grace period her parents had allotted her to get a job, save money, and psychologically prepare for her launch into self-reliance. But Veronica and John supported each other in sticking to the process of A.C.E.S. recovery. Eventually Skylar was forced to move out of her parents' home. Initially, she stayed with a friend who was willing to allow Skylar to sleep on her couch for a few weeks.

Finally, Skylar contacted her dad, Patrick, and asked to move in with him. Patrick, like Veronica, also felt tremendous guilt for all he put Skylar through as a child so he allowed Skylar to move in with him. After about six months, Patrick began to regret his decision to allow his daughter to move in without having established any pre-conditions. He mistakenly allowed Skylar to simply "hang out" for six months and made all the same errors in judgment that Veronica and John had made over the years. Finally, Patrick insisted Skylar get a job or she would be forced to move out. Taking some advice from his ex-wife, Patrick gave his daughter 30 days' notice to move out! This time, Skylar was able to recognize that she was out of options if she didn't want to be homeless.

Skylar found a job at a large retail book store. Although she earned a very modest wage, she worked full-time and was able to pay her father a reasonable amount of money for rent and other living expenses. She saved some money and bought a used car which was a nice upgrade from walking and taking the bus. Most importantly, as a result of being given a dose of reality, Skylar finally became a self-supporting adult.

As if A.C.E.S. Wasn't Enough!

Skylar's family illustrates the dilemma of A.C.E.S. when it exists alongside other psychological and emotional disorders. The presence of one or more psychological disorders such as depression, anxiety, addictions, co-dependency, or post-traumatic stress disorder, in addition to a primary disorder, such as A.C.E.S., is known as *co-morbidity* or *co-occurring* disorders within the psychiatric and psychological communities.

Co-occurring disorders, including disorders paired with A.C.E.S., demand special consideration in terms of applying standard recovery processes.

Many psychiatric illnesses such as Major Depression, Generalized Anxiety Disorder, Mood Disorders Due to a General Medical Condition (such as hormonal imbalances), Post-traumatic Stress Disorder, and Addictive Disorders tend to run in families. If there is a history of mental illness in your family and you have already determined that your family is suffering from A.C.E.S., it may be a good idea to see a psychiatrist for a complete psychiatric evaluation. Family members may need medical treatment before being able to tolerate the emotional demands that the A.C.E.S. recovery process imposes. The following is a brief breakdown of some psychiatric disorders that are frequently diagnosed in A.C.E.S. family members.

Major Depressive Disorder

Major depressive disorder, otherwise known as clinical depression, is often confused with "the blues" or situational sadness. Major depressive disorder is very different from a bout of situational despair. It is a psychiatric disorder that often requires medical intervention. Mood disorders, such as Major depressive disorder, are common among families with A.C.E.S. and can become debilitating if not properly treated. Clinical symptoms of depression may be expressed by feelings of helplessness, diminished self-directed activity, poor concentration (vital when trying to complete tasks such as filling out job applications or studying), negative thoughts (in the form of a defeatist attitude), difficulty performing simple tasks (such as getting up at a regular time of day), attending to personal grooming, lethargy, the desire to isolate, anger, irritability and general despair. Perhaps you have seen your own adult-child exhibit these symptoms of clinical depression. In A.C.E.S. families, parents of adult-children could easily become confused when trying to determine whether their adult-children are suffering from clinical depression or are simply exhibiting the effects of A.C.E.S.!

If an A.C.E.S. family member is indeed suffering from major depression you may be wondering how to determine what ought to be addressed first, the depression or A.C.E.S. If A.C.E.S. seems to be *causing* the depression, it seems logical that recovery from A.C.E.S. would cure the depression. While A.C.E.S. recovery is likely to trigger a multitude of positive reactions, it is not at all likely to cure a medical condition like major depression. Clinically diagnosable depression needs to be addressed medically and psychologically. You may be able to initiate the A.C.E.S. recovery process concurrently with depression treatment, but it would be a mistake to assume the depression will subside without direct medical and psychological intervention. Incidentally, the depression will need to be actively managed in order for the A.C.E.S. recovery process to succeed. Recovery from A.C.E.S. requires a lot of emotional energy. Major depression drains emotional energy to the point where most people would not have enough of a reserve left to meaningfully participate in the A.C.E.S. recovery process.

The logical first step in dealing with co-occurring disorders, such as major depression and A.C.E.S., is to obtain a psychiatric evaluation given by a board certified *Psychiatrist*, not a *General Practitioner* who may not be fully aware of all the latest psychopharmacology available to physicians treating mental illness. If a prescription treatment plan is indicated, the depressed individual can begin medical treatment for the depression immediately. It may also be appropriate for the depressed family member to receive psychotherapy to address and resolve emotional issues associated with the depression. It may not be possible to have perfect concurrence in terms of A.C.E.S. recovery and depression treatment, but once the depression is on the road to manageability, the A.C.E.S. recovery process should begin in earnest.

Generalized Anxiety Disorder (GAD)

Most everyone experiences anxiety from time to time. It is perfectly normal for anxiety to occur when we are nervous, worried, or concerned about particular events, circumstances, and so forth. The key word in the previous sentence is "occur" which means that anxious feelings naturally *occur* in response to *specific* factors. A diagnosable anxiety disorder is different from the kind of anxiety a person may experience before interviewing for a job, for instance. Clinical anxiety disorders significantly interfere with peoples' overall level of day-to-day functioning to varying degrees and are not specific to single events, such as a job interview as mentioned above.

The *Diagnostic Statistical Manual-IV-tr (DSM-IV-tr)* is the standard written source of information on all diagnosable psychiatric illnesses. The

DSM-IV-tr focuses on diagnostic criteria, empirical research, and provides credible education for clinical practice. It contains all such information for some 12 distinct anxiety disorders including GAD. If you are interested in reviewing an exhaustive description of the 12 different anxiety disorders classified by the DSM-IV-tr, you can purchase a copy at most bookstores or from an online book seller. Anxiety, as it pertains to A.C.E.S., will be addressed in general terms for the purpose of brevity and to illustrate applicability.

A.C.E.S. family members regularly experience *manageable* feelings of anxiety. But some A.C.E.S. family members may experience truly unmanageable feelings of anxiety which could legitimately interfere with the A.C.E.S. recovery process. When that is the case, it would be wise to medically and psychologically address the anxiety disorder directly so that the A.C.E.S. recovery process (which requires all family members to make emotional and behavioral changes) can proceed. A.C.E.S. recovery should never be emotionally or psychologically *intolerable* for the anxiety-disordered family member.

As a rule, *most* A.C.E.S. family members have difficulty with change. While they may be consciously aware of, and frustrated by, the monotony they experience within their family-systems, they resist making the kinds of changes that would alter the status quo. Most obviously in A.C.E.S. families, adult-children resist moving out and taking responsibility for themselves. In complementary fashion, parents enable perpetual dependency to avoid making changes. And spouses in A.C.E.S. families allow their marriages to decompensate by refusing to change the dysfunctional ways in which they relate to one another.

In A.C.E.S. families, anxiety seems to present itself in predictable ways. For example, an A.C.E.S. mother with GAD may experience intense anxiety when she imagines her adult-child attempting to provide for himself on his own. Having little to no confidence her child can successfully become independent, she may visualize her child homeless and starving. In all likelihood, a mom like this would overwhelm herself with feelings of guilt for wanting to kick her adult-son out of the house. She would probably ruminate over the *horrible things* that could happen to him if she were to do so. In order to stave off her own anxiety, she would continue to tolerate the unacceptable entitled attitude and immature behavior of her adult-child. In short, her anxiety would cause her to undermine the A.C.E.S. recovery process.

An A.C.E.S. parent with GAD who is attempting to maintain constant contact with her adult-child is a representative example of anxiety-driven behavior. Such a parent may phone or text-message her adult-child constantly to make sure she is all right. This behavior, in all probability, will lead to the development of an unhealthy emotional dependency for both parties. The adult-child may also form inappropriate feelings of responsibility to manage her parent's anxiety by repressing her own healthy desire to assume an independent lifestyle.

The parent in the above example may be excessively preoccupied with worry about her adult-child. She may require constant reassurance about her adult-child's welfare in order to feel in control. She may sit up at night waiting for her son or daughter to walk through the front door, unable to sleep until her adult-child is safely home. This is not normal behavior, even for a parent in an A.C.E.S. family! It may represent a diagnosable anxiety disorder that needs to be addressed medically.

Adult-children may also exhibit symptoms of diagnosable anxiety disorders in a variety of ways. One common example of debilitating anxiety among adult-children in A.C.E.S. families is a fear of driving which can severely impede independence, particularly in some parts of the country where public transportation is virtually unavailable.

A frequently diagnosed anxiety disorder for A.C.E.S. adult-children is *Agoraphobia (see the DSM-IV-tr for a complete description of Agoraphobia)*, which is a fear of crowds, public places, or a generalized fear of leaving the house. Clearly, if a person is afraid to leave the house, finding a job, going to school, or moving out of the family home would be extraordinarily difficult!

Fortunately, GAD (and other diagnosable anxiety disorders) can usually be well-managed via medical and psychological interventions. Once the anxiety is under control the A.C.E.S. recovery process can and should proceed.

Mood Disorders Due to a General Medical Condition

Low Testosterone (Low-T), Pre-menstrual Syndrome (PMS), Pre-menstrual Dysphoric Disorder (PMDD), and Menopause can all wreak havoc on peoples' psychological, emotional, and physical stability. All of these disorders are related to hormonal imbalances and can actually impede the A.C.E.S. recovery process if not directly addressed. The following is a brief breakdown of each of these hormonal conditions.

Low Testosterone (Low-T)

Adult-males may sometimes develop a condition known as Low Testosterone (Low-T). Its symptoms include low-energy, decreased sex drive, and anhedonia (the inability to enjoy regularly enjoyable activities) among others. If you do a simple Internet search on Low-T and follow it up with a search for a list of the symptoms of clinical depression, you will find that there is considerable overlap between the two symptom profiles. A.C.E.S. fathers/husbands who suspect they may be experiencing the symptoms of Low-T (or depression for that matter) may want to check with their doctors to identify the specific age of onset for the disorder. Doctors may order blood tests to determine hormonal levels in order to diagnose or rule out Low-T. If an A.C.E.S. father/husband is found to have this treatable condition, he may want to consider receiving medical treatment to manage his hormonal imbalance. With Low-T under control, he may be better equipped to carry on with the A.C.E.S. recovery process. Fathers/husbands play a critical role in the overall A.C.E.S. recovery process. They will learn much more about that in Chapter 2 of Part II.

Menopause, Pre-menstrual Syndrome (PMS) and Pre-menstrual Dysphoric Disorder (PMDD)

Menopause is a normal condition that all women experience as they age. The term "menopause" is commonly used to describe any of the changes a woman experiences either just before or after she stops menstruating, marking the end of her reproductive years. Many women report significantly disruptive physical and emotional symptoms during menopause including severe mood swings.

PMS and PMDD are similar to one another but there is a significant distinction between the two disorders. PMS is certainly unpleasant in terms of its physical and emotional symptoms, but it is not nearly as disruptive as PMDD. The DSM-IV-tr refers to Pre-menstrual Dysphoric Disorder (PMDD) as a severe form of PMS that causes physical and mood-related symptoms that can seriously disrupt a woman's life and negatively impact her relationships.

PMDD symptoms could reasonably be compared to symptoms of major depression or Generalized Anxiety Disorder (GAD). Emotional symptoms include feelings of sadness, hopelessness, anxiety, irritability, emotional sensitivity, anger, feeling overwhelmed, and a desire to withdraw from others. Physical and behavioral symptoms include a lack of energy, problems with concentrating, sleep problems, food cravings or binge eating, breast tenderness, bloating and weight gain, headaches, and joint or muscle pain. With the exception of breast tenderness and bloating, all of the aforementioned symptoms could be attributed to major depression or GAD. Hence, the hormonal shifts brought about by menopause, PMS or PMDD may likewise interfere with the A.C.E.S. recovery process.

If a woman in a family with A.C.E.S. is dealing with Menopause, PMS or PMDD, she should consider consulting her gynecologist to learn whether medical intervention is indicated and then decide whether or not to follow through on the recommendations of her doctor. Working through the A.C.E.S. recovery process is hard enough! Trying to do it when one's hormonal levels are fluctuating wildly from day to day could make the process more difficult than it needs to be.

If you suspect that you or a family member is struggling with a Mood Disorder Due to a General Medical Condition such as Low-T, Menopause, PMS or PMDD, it should be addressed as soon as possible, whether your family is ready to begin the A.C.E.S. recovery process or not.

Post-traumatic Stress Disorder

I would like to provide readers with a brief description of Post-traumatic Stress Disorder (PTSD) which is present (to varying degrees) in many A.C.E.S. family members. PTSD is a severe psychological disorder that is brought on by extremely traumatic events or situations that involve terrifying or tremendously shocking situations (such as the sudden death of a parent or child). The characteristic symptoms of the disorder may appear immediately or long after exposure to traumatic stressors depending on many factors such as age of the victim, how the aftermath of the trauma is addressed or not addressed, and various other circumstances.

People with PTSD often describe the feelings they experienced during their traumas in a similar way. They recall feelings of intense fear, feelings of helplessness, and feelings of horror (as in witnessing a murder, for example). Some symptoms of PTSD include recurrent and intrusive memories of the event, upsetting dreams about the event, flashbacks (i.e., a feeling of re-experiencing the event), and extreme distress at exposure to internal or external cues which trigger memories of the event. Many people with PTSD experience physiological reactions to triggers as well. These physical symptoms include rapid heartbeat, increased perspiration, or feelings of physical weakness.

The DSM-IV-tr (*Diagnostic Statistical Manual-IV-tr*) provides a complete overview of PTSD for readers interested in a more exhaustive description of the disorder.

With regards to A.C.E.S., PTSD is frequently present within the marital-unit of families with A.C.E.S. Sadly, one or sometimes both members of the marital-unit may be suffering from PTSD which developed as a result of an abusive or otherwise traumatic childhood. For our purpose, we will consider the impact of emotional and/or physical neglect, physical violence, sexual abuse, and overwhelming shock on the development of PTSD in families with A.C.E.S. We will then recognize the relationship between the presence of PTSD and the exacerbation of the A.C.E.S. family dilemma.

Surviving an abusive childhood is highly likely to produce major emotional disturbances as well as a relentless *preoccupation with self.*

Preoccupation with self, which is born out of a belief that one will not be taken care of by others, can manifest into selfish behavior and attitudes on the part of the person. Since the person believes that no one cares about his feelings or needs, he concludes that he must meet his needs himself. If the person is suffering from PTSD as a result of traumatic stressors in his childhood, he may have rationalized his need to be selfish since even his most profound need for protection was not met when he was a child. With this faulty belief system in place, he focuses his energy on meeting his own needs which may in turn cause him to neglect the needs of others. Without the benefit of context, most people would find his behaviors and attitudes selfish and self-centered.

Excessive devotion to self is the definition of selfishness. Selfish people are concerned primarily with their own interests, benefits, welfare, etc., regardless of the needs of others. But it is my contention that selfish people are not being selfish to intentionally hurt those they love. Rather they are overcome with fear that they will not get what they want or have what they need. Therefore, selfishness is a mere manifestation of fear. Specifically, selfish people seem to have a profound, albeit sub-conscious, fear of death and dying.

That may sound like an overstatement of the highest order! You may be thinking, *"So if I'm selfish it's because I'm afraid of dying?"* Yes, but let me explain the relationship between selfish behavior and fear of dying. As children, we believe that we will die if our needs go unmet. And when basic needs such as food and shelter go unmet, young children will indeed die.

Since our parents are the people who typically provide for us our basic needs, we naturally expect that they will provide for *all* of our needs including our genuine need for love and affection. As very young children, we are not able to discern which unmet need will cause us to die. As rational adults we realize that we are not likely to die if we feel we are not getting enough love and affection. But for small children, who are unable to rationalize feelings, it may feel as though they will. So when parents fall short of meeting intangible needs, such as love and affection, a latent fear of dying ensues and we intervene on our *own* behalves. The fear of death activates our instinct of self-preservation and triggers a lasting preoccupation with self which oftentimes manifests into selfish behaviors and attitudes.

Let's look at an example of how a parent with PTSD can interfere with the A.C.E.S. recovery process. Let's say the mother in an A.C.E.S. family was frequently beaten by her father whenever her mother and siblings were out of the house. On a subconscious or conscious level, she may fear being left alone with anyone who could conceivably hurt her (e.g., her husband). She may undermine her adult-child's attempts to move out so that she won't have to tolerate anxious feelings about being alone with her husband. But her behavior is incredibly selfish, as she is placing her imagined needs over her adult-child's legitimate need to progress in life.

Let's look at one more illustration of how PTSD can interfere with the A.C.E.S. recovery process. Let's say a father in an A.C.E.S. family was badly neglected in childhood. His parents did not consistently meet his basic needs. Many times he was left to get food on his own. The heat in his house would often be shut off for non-payment of the monthly utility bill for gas. His clothes were ill fitting and were not properly laundered. He never had any money for anything. At 15 he moved out of the house and lived with friends and relatives for months at a time. As a father in an A.C.E.S. family, he may feel extreme internal conflict whenever trying to hold his adult-child to reasonable expectations for responsible behavior. Wanting his child to have everything he did not, this A.C.E.S father may over-indulge his adult-child, enabling his son or daughter to develop a debilitating sense of entitlement. The father may feel unable to say "no" to his adult-child. He may visualize his adult-child struggling to support herself in the real world where he cannot protect her from harm. The father may want to avoid re-experiencing painful memories of when he had no one to rely upon other than himself and might end up rescuing his daughter needlessly, preventing her from achieving her independence as an adult.

If A.C.E.S. parents suffered from neglect or emotional, physical, or sexual abuse in childhood, they might meet the criteria for a clinical diagnosis of PTSD. PTSD in a family member has the potential to completely block the A.C.E.S. recovery process and should be addressed without delay.

Addictions

Active addiction can, and often does, devastate otherwise happy families. Anyone who has lived with an addicted family member can tell you that it is unpredictable, intensely disappointing, anxiety producing, and emotionally exhausting. Active addiction naturally commands attention within family-systems and inhibits the nurturing of healthy inter-familial relationships.

Addictions such as alcohol dependency, drug addiction, eating disorders, and self-mutilation (e.g.., cutting or burning the skin) create so much havoc in households that everything seems to stop in order to keep the addicted person alive and functional. For example, marital relationships suffer immeasurable damage when couples expend enormous quantities of emotional energy on their addicted sons or daughters. The chronic drain on their emotional energy causes spouses to neglect their marriages. If an A.C.E.S. parent is the addict, an adult-child may feel obligated to look after his drunken mother, drug addicted father, or morbidly obese parent whose health has badly deteriorated as a result of his or her compulsive overeating.

Clearly, addictions must be dealt with directly and resolutely. Limits must be set with addicts and those limits *must be honored* by those who set them. To not follow through on ultimatums (e.g., "If you get drunk one more time, I'm throwing you out") will only lead to lost credibility with the addict. Addicts usually need to learn things the hard way if they are to recover from their addictions, whatever they may be. As a Nationally Certified Master Addiction Counselor, I can tell you that I have never seen a single case where an addict has achieved anything like long-term abstinence or sobriety if he or she never had to suffer any meaningful consequences for his or her addictive behavior.

Once an addiction has been identified in an A.C.E.S. family member, that family must formulate a realistic plan to deal with the situation and the plan needs to be enacted as quickly as possible. The plan must clearly outline consequences for destructive addictive behavior on the part of the addict and enabling on the part of other family members. If addicts fail to take action to arrest their addictions (as is likely in cases where addicts are not ready to recover) then the consequences MUST BE ENFORCED!

Once addiction has been managed or neutralized via natural consequences, the A.C.E.S. recovery program should begin.

Cyclical infidelity

Cyclical infidelity, or a recurring pattern of unfaithfulness to one's spouse, operates the same way as any other behavioral addiction. It begins as a vehicle to escape one's reality. Cheaters describe experiencing a "high" that comes from keeping their affairs secret from their spouses. And cyclical cheaters often describe time spent with their secret lovers as euphoric and thrilling.

As with any other addiction, the addictive cycle for recurring infidelity begins and progresses with astonishing predictability. First, tension builds in the life of the "cheater". Next, he or she acts out with addictive behavior (e.g., pursuit of an extramarital affair) to relieve the tension. He or she will then experience temporary gratification. Ordinarily, if the addictive behavior results in negative consequences, he or she will experience regret and remorse. Typically, he or she will then decide to (or will be commanded to) abstain from the addictive behavior. Then a "honeymoon" phase will ensue when the marital relationship begins to heal. Once the threat of severe consequences (such as a divorce) has been abated, tension will build again and, lastly, the cycle will repeat.

I've chosen to explain cyclical infidelity in its own sub-section of this chapter because of two unique characteristics which separate it from other addictions. First, cyclical infidelity triangulates another human being into the marriage via the addictive process. Second, cyclical infidelity has the potential to devastate marriages in a way no other addiction does. That is not to say that active alcoholism, drug addiction, compulsive gambling, etc., are not capable of ruining marriages. But unlike other addictions which are recognized as diagnosable mental diseases, "cheating" is something a lot of people consider to be an issue of character. Alcoholism, for example, is a disease from which people can recover. It is generally understood that developing alcoholism is not intentional; that once addicted, people may actually come to drink against their will. But infidelity is seen as a conscious decision that results in the shattering of another's ability to trust. And for many people, cheating is an unforgivable act that cannot be reconciled.

However, when cyclical cheating occurs in a family with A.C.E.S., it does *not* typically result in a decision to divorce.

So what could cause the marital-unit in an A.C.E.S. family to stay together in spite of cyclical infidelity? There is one specific motivational factor, consistent with the classical characteristics of A.C.E.S. families, which facilitates the atypical decision to stay together in spite of cyclical infidelity: triangulation.

In Chapter 4 of Part I we explored the concept of triangulation and its presence in A.C.E.S. families. In these families, adult-children are recruited into their parents' marriages and are used to diffuse emotional tension between the spouses. Secret lovers in extra-marital affairs are also used to diffuse marital tension. A.C.E.S. spouses may seek out extra-marital affairs in an attempt to get their emotional needs met and to escape intra-marital despair.

Particularly in situations where the adult-child is the opposite sex of the cheated-on parent, the cheated-on parent may be reliant on the adult-child for spouse-like emotional support. She (the cheated-on parent), for instance, could seriously undermine her adult-child's ability to become independent in order to keep her source of emotional support in the household. Complementarily, the adult-child may use the situation to justify dependency. For example, the adult-child may convince himself that he would be abandoning his mother if he were to "leave her".

As explained in the previous sub-section on addiction, it is important that marital-units in A.C.E.S. families address and eliminate cyclical infidelity rather than "use" their adult-children to supplement their emotional needs. Spouses must seek to have their emotional needs met without reliance on cyclical cheating and certainly without undermining their adult-child's ability to become a fully-functioning, independent adult.

Chapter Summary

Co-occurring disorders are not uncommon in families with A.C.E.S. Before beginning the A.C.E.S. recovery program it would be wise to have a professional diagnostician (e.g., a psychiatrist, psychotherapist, addiction specialist, or medical doctor) identify or rule out the presence of disorders that could negatively interfere with your family's recovery from A.C.E.S.

Oftentimes, after successful treatment of commonly identified co-occurring disorders, A.C.E.S. families can experience rapid A.C.E.S. recovery. Additionally, once legitimate co-occurring disorders are identified and properly addressed, A.C.E.S. family members may be able to replace feelings of resentment with feelings of compassion and understanding for one another, both of which are critical facets of the A.C.E.S. recovery program.

Chapter 6 – A.C.E.S. and the Adult-child with Special Needs

Case Study #3 – Mary, Margaret and Peter

Margaret and Peter came to see me when their daughter, Mary, was 32 years old. They had been married for 34 years. They had a 33 year-old son named Mark who lived with his wife and children in another state. Mary had lived with Margaret and Peter all her life.

Mary was born with a neurodevelopmental disorder that interfered with her ability to manage impulses and emotions. Mary had a difficult time relating to people outside of her immediate family and either completely withdrew from strangers or became aggressive when she came into contact with them. If she felt that she wasn't getting her point across when trying to communicate, she would become very frustrated and angry and could even become violent. She was also mildly retarded.

Margaret and Peter learned everything they could about Mary's condition and did whatever was indicated to help her function to the best of her ability. With a lot of help from therapists, teachers, doctors, and her parents, Mary was able to tend to most of her personal needs without direct assistance. She was also able to follow simple directions and learned to use behavioral skills to help manage her interpersonal difficulties.

While Mary's limitations were substantial, they were not so debilitating as to require constant care. But Margaret and Peter underestimated Mary's ability to function independently. That is not to say that Mary didn't require some help in managing her disabilities, but Margaret and Peter made it a full-time occupation. They believed that they were the only ones who truly understood their daughter. They were reluctant to take advice from the professionals that worked with Mary. Doctors, therapists, and teachers counseled them to let Mary develop her ability to function more independently. But Margaret and Peter discounted the collective counsel of these professionals, believing they knew what was best for their daughter.

Mary accompanied Margaret and Peter nearly everywhere they went. Even when Mary had opportunities to spend time with friends or relatives, Margaret and Peter preferred that their daughter be with them.

About a year ago, Mary's psychiatrist told Margaret and Peter that their daughter appeared to be depressed. He suggested that perhaps she needed more diversion and recommended that she go to a weekday occupational therapy program which would allow Mary to mix with peers, have diversions, learn working skills, and develop a sense of independence. Margaret and Peter became angry at the doctor. They believed the doctor was somehow accusing them of causing Mary's depression. Assuring them that he was accusing no such thing, this intuitive doctor asked them to consider whether they might also be depressed. When Margaret became almost immediately tearful, the doctor knew he'd struck a nerve. He suggested that Margaret and Peter see a family therapist to help figure out the source of their 'family-depression'.

When Margaret and Peter came to see me I could see that they were irritable and burned-out. They admitted they were not happy. When I asked about their marital relationship, they shrugged which seemed to convey that they hadn't really ever thought about the state of their relationship.

Margaret and Peter seemed to talk about Mary incessantly. I needed to redirect them numerous times each session to help them stay focused on other topics. As they shared their history with me, it became evident that Mary was triangulated in their relationship. I explained the concept of triangulation to Margaret and Peter. They seemed interested in the concept and quickly recognized how it pertained to their family.

As I delved further into the history of Margaret and Peter's relationship, I learned that the foundation for their marriage was shaky. They decided to marry when Margaret discovered she was three months pregnant with their son, Mark. The wedding was rushed and neither of them felt prepared for marriage. They really didn't know each other very well and would have preferred to date a few more years before getting engaged. Getting pregnant with their son out of wedlock was an accident but neither wanted to give the baby up for adoption or have an abortion. They wanted to give their baby a two-parent home so they decided to get married and make a go of it.

Their first year of their marriage was eventful, to say the least. They bought a house. Their son was born. And three months after Mark's birth, they found that they were expecting Mary. After Mary was born, they were so busy and overwhelmed with everything that they practically lost track of each other in the day-to-day hustle and bustle. There was one thing that seemed to bring them together and that was the shared feeling of responsibility they had for Mary's welfare.

Mary was a stay-at-home mom who threw herself into caring for her two children while Peter worked full-time for the city as a human resources professional.

Peter and Margaret described their son, Mark as "a good boy who wasn't any trouble." Mark was developmentally normal and demonstrated early aptitude for academics and music. They were both very proud of Mark and were gratified to see him happy and successful in his adult life. They claimed to want the same kind of happiness for Mary but explained "… it's not possible for our daughter."

Margaret and Peter's story is familiar to a specific population of A.C.E.S. families. In this population, the A.C.E.S. adult-children don't necessarily maintain an inappropriate sense of entitlement. That is because their parents assure them that they ARE entitled. They see their adult-children as appropriately dependent upon them and intensely resist the process of de-triangulation.

I worked with Margaret and Peter to help them recognize that their marriage needed a drastic overhaul. I also helped them to accept that Mary wasn't nearly as helpless as they had enabled her to become. While it was a very difficult process for them, they eventually were able to let Mary go a bit. She joined an occupational therapy group for the mentally challenged and clearly loved the program. Margaret and Peter saw their daughter thriving in the kind of peer-group environment they could never have provided for her on their own.

With Mary away at her program so many hours each day, Margaret and Peter had a lot more time alone together which actually triggered a lot of anxiety for both of them. They seemed to be very shy around each other and even awkward at times. In counseling sessions, they sometimes seemed like *strangers who wouldn't dream of interrupting each other (i.e., they didn't want to be rude to one another). They realized they didn't have much to say to each other, both assuming they had nothing in common other than their children.*

I had each of them do a personal inventory to find out exactly what they would like to do if they didn't have to take care of Mary constantly. I asked them not to share their lists with each other until we convened at our next counseling session. What we discovered was that they both wanted to pursue activities geared towards personal development. The activities were not necessarily the same, but they both had a desire to grow. Margaret wanted to learn to play the guitar. Peter had always wanted to learn how to speak Spanish. Margaret wanted to learn cook Chinese food. Peter wanted to volunteer his time with a literacy program for adults. Margaret wanted to teach Catechism for children at her parish church. Peter wanted to get his real estate license! As it turned out, both Margaret and Peter had many interests to pursue which would give them a lot to share with each other. We were even able to identify a couple of interests they could pursue together.

Margaret and Peter learned a lot about each other throughout the A.C.E.S. recovery process. They found that they had come to truly love and appreciate each other over the years.

As is often the case with special-needs-adult-children, Mary continued to live with her parents. But through the A.C.E.S. recovery process, the intrafamilial status quo was drastically altered for the better. The spouses began to function like a healthy marital-unit. And, while she continued to require some help from her parents, Mary was allowed to develop her spirit of independence! The attitude in the household became positive and hopeful with all members assuming their proper roles in the family-unit.

A.C.E.S. Recovery does not Discriminate!

While this book is primarily directed to A.C.E.S. families with healthy adult-children (i.e., without permanent mental or physical disabilities), I felt it might be helpful to write a brief chapter for A.C.E.S. families with special-needs-adult-children.

It's important to understand the distinction between adult-children with circumstantial problems and special-needs-adult-children with permanent disabilities. I would consider active addiction, for example, a circumstantial problem. That is because addiction recovery can almost always be achieved by addicts that are earnestly motivated to recover. While it is my contention that addictions are serious illnesses that often need to be addressed medically, psychologically, emotionally and spiritually, they should not be classified as permanent disabilities. Special-needs-adult-children have chronic mental illnesses, pervasive developmental disorders, or physical disabilities that persist throughout their lives.

The same sorts of predictors that A.C.E.S. will develop in families without disabled adult-children exist in families with special-needs-adult-children. Exceptions to the rule occur when special-needs-adult-children suffer from profound mental retardation or severe mental or physical illnesses. These exceptions will be addressed later in this chapter.

Adult-children, disabled or not, can and should be expected to function as responsible adults and can be raised to live as independently as possible. For example, an adult-child in a wheel chair can learn to negotiate public transportation, job situations, etc., so long as they are thoroughly motivated. Even adult-children with disabilities such as blindness or deafness, can be raised to become fully independent adults provided that special training, education, and appropriate social services are made available to the adult-child.

It is important for parents of special-needs-adult-children to avoid infantilizing them. An adult-child with special needs will have a difficult time maintaining a positive attitude about his ability to care for himself if he's been treated like a helpless individual all his life.

The following is a list of mistakes many A.C.E.S. parents make as they care for their special-needs-adult-children:

1. **Doing for adult-children what they can do for themselves**. When parents opt to perform ordinary tasks for their children instead of facilitating autonomy, they create unhealthy dependency and indoctrinate their children with faulty belief systems that they are unable to care for themselves.

2. **Underestimating capabilities.** If parents underestimate the capabilities of their adult-child, they will undermine their adult-child's ability to feel confident and ultimately decrease her motivation to do without assistance.

3. **Isolation of the adult-child.** When disabled adult-children are under-socialized, they may become overly reliant on their parents for companionship and social interaction.

4. **Total Enmeshment of the adult-child.** Some parents of disabled adult-children tend to go beyond triangulation and may actually come to fully incorporate their children into their marital relationships. Their adult-children may be included in all activities, preventing opportunities for spouses to nurture their marital relationships through quality time spent as a couple.

In general, A.C.E.S. parents of special-needs-adult-children have a very difficult time recognizing and accepting that their adult-children have options regarding how they will live their lives. The parents assume total responsibility for their adult-children, making decisions for them that they could make on their own.

These parents come to depend on their adult-children to legitimize the meaningful purpose in their own lives; i.e., the parents' need to provide excessive care for their adult-children masks their deficiencies in the area of self-actualization.

However, this chapter must responsibly address the importance of delineating the exceptions to the assertion that special-needs-adult-children can and should be expected to become independent adults. As stated earlier, when adult-children are disabled by profound mental retardation, severe mental illness, or physical disabilities so incapacitating as to prevent their ability to care for their basic needs, such as toileting, bathing, dressing, and eating, compassion and tenderness must rule the day. Examples of severe mental illnesses might include Schizophrenia, Schizoaffective disorder, Dissociative Identity Disorder, Bipolar I Disorder (to include random incidences of psychotic mania), and other disorders where chronic or intermittent psychosis is characteristic.

In cases such as the ones listed above, consulting medical and social service professionals who are trained and experienced in how to maximize the functioning of adult-children with these sorts of severe limitations is usually necessary, both for the adult-children and their families.

It should go without saying that special-needs-adult-children with severe limitations require specialized care and consideration. The limits imposed upon them because of their conditions or illnesses are many and A.C.E.S. parents need to be realistic about what their adult-children can and cannot manage.

However, A.C.E.S. parents struggling to care for their special-needs-adult-children can still avoid triangulating them into their relationships, regardless of their limitations. If triangulation has already occurred in a family with a special-needs-adult-child, the adult-child must be encouraged to individuate and the spouses must address their relationship issues or problems within their marital-unit are certain to escalate.

Thankfully, day-treatment programs are usually available in most large cities for special-needs-adult-children. These programs teach coping skills and behavior modification in addition to providing structure and social interaction. They also make it possible for parents of special-needs-adult-children to rest without worrying about the welfare of their adult-children. All caretakers, including A.C.E.S. parents of special-needs-adult-children, need to respect their own limitations and prioritize self-care. The mental, physical, and emotional exhaustion brought about by providing *constant* care is real and comes with certain risks (including the annihilation of romantic energy between A.C.E.S. spouses).

It's very important for spouses in families with special-needs-adult-children to be consciously aware of the signs of "burn-out" in themselves and in each other. Burn-out can actually lead to neglect and abuse of adult-children and should be avoided at all costs.

So what drives the compulsion for A.C.E.S. parents of special-needs-adult-children to insist on being sole providers of day-to-day care for their adult-children? The simple answer is that the parents maintain a faulty belief that no one else could care for their children as effectively as they can. These parents may have a point when it comes to their special ability to administer care with parental love. But this practice causes special-needs-adult-children to become isolated unnecessarily. It prevents them from learning how to function around other people and to realize their full potential.

It's very important for A.C.E.S. parents of special-needs-adult-children to realize that the existing arrangement (in which the parents provide all the care for their special-needs-adult-children) will someday come to an end. Due to the aging process, parents will eventually become unable to care for their adult-children. Those adult-children may be traumatized by changes in their routines, particularly if they've never learned how to adapt to new situations or to caregivers other than their parents. But this kind of trauma can be avoided through the use of social services created to foster flexibility and adaptability in special-needs-adults.

Whenever possible, A.C.E.S. parents need to avoid inhibiting their dependent adult-children from achieving a modicum of independence and confidence. Failure to do so typically creates rigidity and extreme fear of change in adult-children.

The rule of thumb is to proceed thoughtfully and compassionately when assessing how to embark upon the A.C.E.S recovery program if the family includes a special-needs-adult-child.

Chapter Summary

Families that have adult-children with special needs face a unique challenge with regards to A.C.E.S. recovery. Be that as it may, the most critical thing for such families to know is that A.C.E.S. recovery is just as possible, and certainly as beneficial, as it is to typical A.C.E.S. families. A.C.E.S. recovery is in the best interest of *every* family member, including those adult-children with special needs. Recognizing that some special-needs-adult-children have real and measurable limitations in terms of accomplishing total personal responsibility, families (specifically marital-units) can almost always eliminate or reduce interpersonal dysfunction through the A.C.E.S. recovery process.

Many A.C.E.S. parents of special-needs-adult-children struggle with feelings of guilt when taking their focus off their adult-children in order to more fully attend to the problems in their marriages. These feelings are generally irrational and can actually help A.C.E.S. spouses justify inappropriate and unhealthy marital behavior.

Every adult-child deserves the opportunity to experience his or her personal best when it comes to independent living. Respect for the individual, regardless of his or her limitations, must rule the day. And for special-needs-adult-children, these limitations must always be thoughtfully considered and honored.

Part II

The Remedy for A.C.E.S.: You CAN do This!

Chapter 1 – Phase 1: How to Launch Your Adult-child into the World of Personal Responsibility in 12 Steps

This chapter is a step-by-step guide families can follow to achieve freedom from A.C.E.S. Success is dependent on a firm commitment to the process. This is not a "pick-and-choose" list from which to select the things that are the least uncomfortable for you to execute. The process is one that builds upon itself with two specific goals. The first goal is to launch your adult-child into the world to care for herself within a time period of approximately 12 to 18 months. The second goal is to establish healthy family relationships, particularly between you and your spouse.

There are 12 steps in this process, some of which can and ought to be done concurrently. In this chapter we will look closely at each of the 12 steps. Study this chapter carefully as it is the roadmap to launching your adult-child into the world with a sense of personal responsibility rather than a sense of entitlement.

> *STEP 1: The first step in the A.C.E.S. recovery process is for spouses to become united in their commitment to overcome A.C.E.S.*

The first step in the A.C.E.S. recovery process is for spouses to become united in their commitment to overcome A.C.E.S. This is easier said than done. As previously discussed in Part I, if an adult-child is fully triangulated into a marital-unit, one or both parents may resist a forced launch. Remember, in A.C.E.S. families one or both parents have become inappropriately reliant on the adult-child to help discharge marital stress. Adult-children may have been inappropriately relied upon by one or both parents for emotional support and companionship. Some A.C.E.S. parents may fear feelings of grief and loss when thinking about their adult-child being forced from the family home. Doubt over their adult-child's ability to survive a forced launch may grip A.C.E.S. parents with fear and cause them to withhold their complete commitment to the recovery process.

I cannot stress strongly enough how important it is that marital-units be wholly committed to the A.C.E.S. recovery process. Spouses will need to rely upon each other for support as they approach each new step in the recovery process. Some steps will be easier to apply than others but each and every step must be taken. You cannot skip any part of this process. Only the program in its entirety will deliver your family from A.C.E.S.

Possibly the biggest mistake marital-units could make is to begin the A.C.E.S. recovery process in a half-hearted way. If either partner is wishy-washy about why recovery is necessary, then he or she is not yet willing to commit to the process and will consciously or subconsciously undermine its ability to be successful. Beginning the process without a genuine commitment from both partners to see the process through could very likely ruin a *future* opportunity for A.C.E.S. recovery. That is to say that A.C.E.S. parents are certain to lose credibility with their adult-children if they quit the process half-way through. It would be far better for an A.C.E.S. marital-unit to wait until both partners believe that the A.C.E.S. recovery process is the best way for their family to move forward in a healthy way than for them to begin the process prematurely.

After explaining step one to my A.C.E.S. clients, they often ask how to force readiness when don't yet *feel* ready to begin A.C.E.S. recovery. In other words, they are *willing* to be willing but they are still *not* willing!

The answer is simple. Couples must not confuse readiness with resoluteness. What we are after is a joint resolution to triumph over A.C.E.S.! Step one requires a conjoint commitment to the recovery process. Commitment and resolute essentially mean the same thing. Spouses may not feel *ready* to begin the process. That's normal. Change can be highly intimidating and unnerving and some A.C.E.S. marital-units may *never* be *ready* to make changes that could be uncomfortable. Fortunately, one doesn't have to be ready to be resolute. The question partners need to ask each other is, "Can we be resolute about our commitment to A.C.E.S. recovery regardless of our *feelings* about not being ready?"

By now you can see that A.C.E.S. recovery requires family members to make positive changes. If A.C.E.S. marital-partners are at least able to understand and accept that basic requisite, they can begin this challenging, but critical process.

> **STEP 2: Step two calls for A.C.E.S. spouses to learn and establish healthy communication patterns with one another.**

Step two calls for A.C.E.S. spouses to learn and establish healthy communication patterns with one another. This is a very challenging step for spouses who have been communicating ineffectively for decades. Remember, in A.C.E.S. families, healthy communication necessitates the de-triangulation of the adult-child. Spouses will be required to communicate directly with one another without reliance upon an intermediary to diffuse, re-phrase, alter, or impose the messages meant for each other.

It may be helpful or even necessary for some couples to work directly with a marriage therapist who is very skilled at teaching communication skills in order for them to be successful in step two. Listening is more than half of healthy communication. It is my personal contention that understanding ought to be our goal when engaging in a conversation about anything. When we seek more to understand our partners than to be understood by them, we usually come away with good feeling. We ought to avoid the tendency to impatiently wait for our partners to finish speaking so we can make our own points. Good communication requires us to be C.O.A.L.: Curious, Open-minded, Accepting and Loving.

Curious refers to our sincere desire to understand the perspective of our partners. Curiosity represents a genuine desire to understand the thought process of our partners and may even allow us to marvel, without judgment, about the differences in our positions.

Open-mindedness refers to the need to be *willing* to see your partner's point of view. That does not mean that you will be agreeing with your partner about whatever it is you are arguing about. The idea is to be *willing* to consider your partner's perspective. You may come to find that there is no longer an argument worth having.

Acceptance refers to judgment. It is very important not to judge your partner's point of view from a position of authority or superiority. We can always tell when we are being judged by our partners. Judgment gets our "backs up" and we become more locked into our own positions, making it very difficult to reach middle ground. Bear in mind that judgment is merely an expression of *opinion.* Everyone is entitled to his or her opinion. Acceptance will allow us to tolerate the opinions of others without resentful disdain.

Loving, in the context of C.O.A.L., refers to warmth and tenderness. We offer love to those we regard as precious in our lives. Loving has much to do with joyful sacrifice. Joyful sacrifice is the feeling we have when we'd *rather* give than receive. I don't mean that we'd rather give than receive because we want to maintain control in a given relational exchange. I mean we'd rather give because we love so very tenderly.

Let me give you a personal example of joyful sacrifice. After my daughters were born, I was in a lot of pain. Each birth was facilitated by a c-section operation which weakened my stomach muscles considerably. In turn, my loss of muscle strength caused my back to become weak and strained. It was painful any time I had to bend over to lift something, including my tiny newborn babies. But when either of my baby girls cried out from their cribs, I felt a complete lack of resentment over the sacrifice I needed to make in order to tend to their needs. My back could be hurting and I could be exhausted beyond belief, but the tenderness I felt for each of them fueled my ability to sacrifice my legitimate need to rest my back. Sacrificing for them was a joy because I loved them so much. In fact, if a doctor had ordered me to stay in bed when my babies cried (in order to let someone else look after them) *that* would have been a sacrifice. I *wanted* to be the one to help them. I cherished my precious newborn babies so much! I felt joyful (*and tired!*) when doing things for them.

Now I don't want to give the impression that I was anything like a perfectly selfless mother. I struggled like every new mother does to find the energy to look after the endless needs of her baby. I was really tired and overwhelmed and I'm sure I complained a lot about how much work it was to look after my newborns. But the warmth and tenderness I felt for my girls was present even on my most trying days. I certainly was not eager to spring from my bed at three o'clock in the morning to change a dirty diaper, but my love for those two angels made it easier for me to sacrifice virtually anything including sleep, a hot meal, and even the welfare of my aching body.

Certainly most people can appreciate the precious nature of a baby and the warm and tender feelings that come when we care for one. But we seem to struggle enormously when trying to regard our spouse in the same warm and tender style. Ironically, one of the most common terms of endearment between spouses is "Baby" or "Babe"! The problem is that in the midst of unhealthy communication, warmth and tenderness go right out the window just when it's most important. Maintaining loving feelings for our spouse is a vital part of effective communication.

> **STEP 3: Step three requires that spouses work toward healthy emotional detachment from their adult-child while maintaining awareness of the behaviors that reinforce unhealthy emotional dependencies within their triad.**

Like steps one and two, responsibility for the execution of the third step in the A.C.E.S. recovery process also falls upon the marital-unit. At this point it may seem as though the adult-child is not even remotely involved in the recovery process. So far, that does seem to be the case. And there is a reason for that. A.C.E.S. generally takes root long before most spouses realize they have an entitled-adult-child under their roof. Marital-units cultivate the A.C.E.S. dilemma. The adult-children don't plant A.C.E.S. in their families. A.C.E.S. adult-children are simply the *expression* of A.C.E.S. Their inflated sense of entitlement grew out of problems in their parents' marriages. Therefore, A.C.E.S. spouses must each take responsibility for his or her share of the recovery process which is substantial but not disproportionate. These 12 steps require much action on the part of marital-units and appropriately so.

Step three requires that spouses work toward healthy emotional detachment from their adult-child while maintaining awareness of the behaviors that reinforce unhealthy emotional dependencies within their triad. Learning how to detach is serious business. It takes a lot of effort and willingness to be uncomfortable. The members of an A.C.E.S. family have become so accustomed to relating to each another in inappropriate ways that to relate in healthy ways may feel foreign and wrong.

Prior to A.C.E.S. recovery and the application of step three, for example, a marital-unit may have decided to have a date night. Perhaps the spouses planned to go to dinner and a movie, a perfectly ordinary activity for a romantic couple. Their adult-daughter overheard them making their plans. She assumed (since she had no plans of her own for the evening) that she would be included. She began to express her preferences for the restaurant they would go to and the movie they would see. Once the spouses caught on to their daughter's assumption about being brought along on their date, they probably felt a strong emotional pull to include her. They likely felt compelled to save her from feeling disappointment, anger, or hurt feelings. They were certain they wouldn't have been able to tolerate the inappropriate guilt they'd feel for not taking her along. So they immediately changed gears and included their daughter as though that was the plan all along.

Let's examine this example closely. Once the spouses included their adult-daughter to join them on their date, they succeeded only in reinforcing her emotional dependency upon them. Rather than allowing their daughter to manage her own feelings of disappointment, etc., they further incorporated her into their marital relationship because of groundless feelings of obligation. Let me be perfectly clear: couples are not obligated to invite their adult-children to join them on dates.

It is important to understand what was lost in this example of triangulation. The couple missed an opportunity to be emotionally intimate with one another. Sharing a meal with one other person can indeed be an intimate activity. Watching a movie together could also facilitate intimacy depending on each person's reaction to the film. Whatever conscious or unconscious anxiety the spouses felt about being alone with one another was washed away the minute they included their adult-daughter in their plans. That's not a good thing. The spouses missed an opportunity to triumph over their fear of emotional intimacy.

Learning how to emotionally detach from the feelings of others is an essential part of de-triangulation. If the spouses in the example had been able to emotionally detach from their adult-daughter's feelings, they could have enjoyed their evening together without being burdened with feelings of inappropriate sadness or guilt. Had they been able to resist the temptation to invite their daughter along, they could have demonstrated confidence in her ability to manage her own feelings.

A.C.E.S. family members must learn and practice emotional detachment in order for the A.C.E.S. recovery process to succeed. The following is a list of what you need to know in order to practice healthy emotional detachment.

1. Everyone has feelings.
2. Everyone has a right to his or her own feelings.
3. Feelings are never right or wrong – they are utterly subjective.
4. Feelings are not facts but they do shape attitudes and they trigger behaviors.
5. We have no right to thwart another person's growth by "saving them" from their feelings.
6. We have a duty to care for self and we are responsible for our own feelings, attitudes, and actions.
7. Adults have a duty to care for themselves and they are responsible for their own feelings, attitudes, actions and reactions.
8. We have no right to prevent another person from suffering the natural consequences of his or her own actions; doing so would interfere with that person's need to learn and grow.
9. Emotional detachment does not prevent empathy.
10. Emotional detachment allows us to feel empathy without unnecessary destructive and dysfunctional rescuing.

Put simply, everyone in the A.C.E.S. family gets to have his or her feelings. For example, when an adult-child suffers a harsh consequence as a result of a bad decision, his parents must detach from their own pain, worry, fear, etc. in order for their adult-child to experience the negative feelings associated with his consequence so he can learn from his mistake.

He *gets* to feel sadness, guilt, shame, anger, and embarrassment in the same way that he gets to feel joy and pride when he does something right.

Adult-children will NEVER grow up as long as their parents continue to bail them out of their self-made messes. Parents' inability to emotionally detach from their adult-children helps to maintain the dysfunctional status quo in A.C.E.S. families.

To illustrate the opposite of a healthy expression of emotional detachment, let's say that an adult-child has been arrested for drunk driving. If her parents spend thousands of dollars to bail her out of jail because the thought of her in jail is too painful for *them* to tolerate, they would be expressing an unhealthy emotional attachment to their adult-daughter. If their adult-daughter was driving drunk, endangering her life and the lives and properties of others, she really *ought* to sit in jail. That's where she belongs. But most A.C.E.S. parents in a similar situation would unfairly save their adult-child from the natural consequence of her own poor decision.

A.C.E.S. parents would do well not to reinforce the overinflated sense of entitlement maintained by their adult-children by rescuing them from earned consequences. But parents' emotional enmeshment with their adult-children blocks their ability to think rationally. Using the example above, as inappropriate as it may sound and in addition to bailing their adult-daughter out of jail, the parents would probably retain an attorney to defend her in court. They'd drive her wherever she needed to go if her driver's license got revoked. They would continue to support her financially throughout the entire ordeal. And the only thing the parents would have accomplished in doing all of this for their adult-daughter is to strengthen her belief that she is entitled to the things her parents are doing to take care of her. Her sense of entitlement would become more entrenched after a situation like this simply because her parents did not know how to detach from her emotionally.

Emotional detachment does not cause us to stop loving. Its purpose is to save us from making irrational decisions which we tend to do when we submit to our emotions rather than our common sense. When dealing with immature people who are in the habit of creating drama, we must yield to rational thought and common sense when they ask us for help with one of their self-imposed crises.

Look back at the previous example. The parents bailed their adult-daughter out of jail because the thought of her in there was too much for *them* to tolerate. It may have done their adult-daughter a lot of good to sit there and consider how she found herself in jail. Her motivation to change will not surface if she expects her parents to rescue her whenever she gets in a fix. But if her parents can master the art of emotional detachment, she may at last turn inward for solutions to her problems.

> **STEP 4: Adult-child is educated by both parents about A.C.E.S. and is informed that they have decided to aggressively pursue A.C.E.S. recovery.**

Step four can be a little intimidating for A.C.E.S. family parents. They must educate their adult-children about A.C.E.S. and inform them that they have decided to aggressively pursue the A.C.E.S. program of recovery.

When parents in A.C.E.S. families have treated their adult-children as though they were equal partners in their marriages, *laying down the law,* so to speak, is not easy for them. Be that as it may, directly communicating the new regime is mandatory.

In terms of tone and attitude, A.C.E.S. recovery should be presented in a very positive way. It must not be presented as a *how-to-kick-your-kid-out-of-the-house* program! It is about how *families* can recover from a *family* problem. Recovery from A.C.E.S. is a family mission.

Be prepared for your adult-child to be very defensive and possibly hurt. She may feel ganged-up on by you and your spouse. After all, she was triangulated into your marriage by the two of you. She did not triangulate herself! Now, all by yourselves, you have made a decision that will change her life dramatically. Depending on your family's temperament, there may be yelling, crying or even a silent storm. Don't worry. The most important thing has already been done. The adult-child has been introduced to the reality of the family problem of A.C.E.S. and has been informed about your commitment to recovery.

In short order, the adult-child will hopefully come to realize that she is not being blamed for A.C.E.S. The goal is for her (and you) to understand that A.C.E.S. recovery is necessary for all of you to become a healthy family with healthy inter-familial relationships.

Once your adult-child understands that she is not the scapegoat in your unhealthy marriage, she may be more willing to read this book. Alternatively, she might like to purchase *Introduction to A.C.E.S.,* a 30-minute CD that briefly reviews each chapter of this book. The CD may be a helpful tool for adult-children who are particularly skeptical about A.C.E.S. and who may not be too excited to read a whole book on the subject.

> **STEP 5: *The fifth step requires the spouses and their adult-child to develop a highly specific contract. This contract must explicitly outline the plan that will launch the adult-child into the world of personal responsibility.***

The fifth step requires the spouses and their adult-child to develop a detailed contract that explicitly outlines the plan to launch the adult-child into the world of personal responsibility. A good contract should include the following: 1. Timelines, 2. Savings Goals, and 3. Interpersonal Boundaries.

It must be clear to all concerned that defaulting on the contract will result in irreversible consequences. For example, if the adult-child chooses not to follow through on contract requirements, he might find himself behind in terms of being prepared for the launch. He will have lost time, which is impossible to recover. The adult-child may expect that he will be given some extra time to catch up if he is indeed behind. But the marital-unit must hold firm to the contract as contracts are a reality of adult life. Giving an adult-child extra time because he wasted the time he was allotted is to delude him as to the ways of the real world. Contracts are very important. They are tangible boundaries.

If your electricity is going to be cut off on August 1st, for example, because you failed to pay your bill for three straight months, that's *your* problem. It's not the electric company's problem. Representatives from the electric company are not going to come over with oil lamps and flashlights when your lights stop working. They are not going to give you money to help you get the electricity turned on again. Likewise, if your adult-child fails to achieve the milestones that will allow for a smooth transition out of the home, that is *not your problem*. It is his or her problem. And by the way, he or she GETS TO HAVE A PROBLEM! That's life on life's terms. In general, people who are able to accept reality are happier than those who insist on fighting it. Bottom line: ready or not, the launch will take place on the agreed upon date.

This is non-negotiable. The contract will not be modified in order to accommodate irresponsible behavior. Experiencing natural consequences is a necessary part of the A.C.E.S. recovery process. Suffering natural consequences fosters maturity. Rescuing those who don't really need to be rescued fosters dependency and a sense of entitlement.

Parents may offer to help their adult-child formulate a plan for her new life but they must resist nagging, prodding, and intervening if she falls off track. Remember, we want the adult-child to develop a sense of personal responsibility. For example, if parents make it their business to remind their adult-daughter to pay her bills each month, how on earth is she going to remember to do it once she's out of the house?

Timelines

The need for explicit timelines in the launch contract is obvious and does not need explanation. Allow me to offer one bit of guidance though. Be sure the timelines are *realistic*. For example, finding a fulltime job may take more than one week for an adult-child who has never held one before. Holding your adult-child to such a short timeline would be unrealistic. Correspondingly, it would be ridiculous for an adult-child to insist that it will take him several months to find a fulltime job. Practically anyone who is seriously motivated to find a legitimate fulltime job will have one in a reasonable amount of time unless he or she is genuinely inept interpersonally, physically, or mentally.

Adult-children who are still financially dependent on their parents must suspend the silly notion that they have to *enjoy* their jobs. I recently treated a pair of A.C.E.S. parents who told me about their 27 year-old daughter who finally found a fulltime job after looking for one for several months. Unbelievably, the daughter quit the job after just one month because her boss was "picking on her." Fully entrenched in the A.C.E.S. family dilemma, these parents had actually *supported* their daughter's decision to quit her job since she was so unhappy. Wow!!! Had this family been applying the A.C.E.S. program of recovery, the daughter would have been told to simply manage her at-work relationships the best she could and in the meantime look for a different job. But under no circumstances should she have quit her job without securing another job first.

Your adult-child may decide that he wants to be an airline pilot. He could spend the rest of his life looking for a job as an airline pilot, but unless he already graduated from flight school and is licensed to pilot an aircraft, he will never be hired to fly a plane. The goal at this point is not for your adult-child to find his dream job. The goal is for him to find a way to support himself with a respectable job of some sort. Once he is out on his own, he can pursue flight school in his spare time if that is his choice. He cannot be allowed to default on the contract by setting unachievable goals.

Savings Goals

Contractual savings goals need to be written out in black and white. It is absolutely critical to avoid ambiguity at all turns. For example, having a goal to save money is a non-specific goal. A.C.E.S. recovery requires adult-children to identify savings goals that are measurable. For instance, an adult-child may determine that he needs to save $500 for moving costs and $2,500 for two months of living expenses. He wants to save $4,200 to pay off high-interest credit cards before moving out. And he wants to have $5,000 in cash savings before the launch. Those goals are all specific and measurable and would meet the saving goals requirement in the launch contract.

It is important that savings goals be determined via current research about monthly living costs, moving expenses, and miscellaneous. The research must be thorough and realistic vs. lackadaisical and unrealistic. For example, an adult-child with a monthly income of $2,000 should not set her sights on an apartment that rents for $1,000 a month. Adult-children should try to limit their housing expenses to no more than 25% of their monthly incomes in order to avoid going into debt.

Shopping for housing on a modest budget may be difficult for an adult-child who has lived in a home with many luxuries all her life. She probably won't be able to afford a large space. She may have to do without modern appliances, air conditioning, a laundry room, and a parking space of her own. She may not even be able to live entirely on her own. She may need to live with roommates in order to make ends meet. The good news is that if she is willing to be realistic and make a start at personal responsibility, she may eventually be able to afford a lifestyle more similar to the one she enjoyed when her parents supported her.

Under the umbrella of savings goals, it would be wise to identify a reasonable amount of money to set aside as a *prudent reserve fund*. This is money that is never used for anything other than survival. Only in the case of a real emergency should this fund be drawn upon. A separate cash savings account could also be opened and funded monthly for things like new clothes, birthday gifts, or a new computer. The prudent reserve fund should remain essentially untouched.

Interpersonal Boundaries

Identification of interpersonal boundaries is a very important part of launching contracts between adult-children and marital-units in A.C.E.S. families. Inappropriate interpersonal boundaries play a big role in the development and exacerbation of the A.C.E.S. dilemma. Therefore, a contract that outlines emotional ground rules (*i.e., interpersonal boundaries*) is requisite and is also a best practice in preparation for the launch.

Number one on the list of personal boundaries: **DO NOT NAG the adult-child**. It is not the responsibility of the marital-unit to keep the adult-child on track while she is preparing for the launch. She may not be doing much to find a suitable living situation (which is the singular goal of step six in the A.C.E.S. recovery process) and could be falling behind in the preparation for launch timeline. But that is her responsibility. And she must be allowed to suffer the natural consequences of her inaction. Healthy boundaries do not allow for rescuing adult-children who are perfectly capable of helping themselves.

In drawing up the contract, it would probably be very helpful to put in verbiage which clearly states that reminders will not be proffered and should not be expected. That way the family can avoid the dreaded "But You Never Said That" or "Why Didn't You Remind Me?" conversations.

Number two: **DO NOT MAKE UNSOLICITED OFFERS** to the adult-child. If he needs help finding an apartment or researching the cost of this or that, let him ask you. A.C.E.S. recovery calls for the re-establishment of appropriate boundaries between the marital-unit and the adult-child. If your adult-child asks for your guidance, you can feel free to provide it. That scenario would represent an appropriate boundary between an adult-child and his parents. It is entirely appropriate for an adult-child to seek wisdom and guidance from his parents. In contrast, it is entirely inappropriate for parents to interfere in another *adult's* private business and to assume that he needs help to tend to normal adult responsibilities.

Number three: **CEASE DISCLOSING PRIVATE MARITAL INFORMATION TO NON-CONCERNED PARTIES**. Specifically,

I mean that spouses should not disclose information about their marital relationship to their adult-children and adult-children should not disclose personal information about their personal business to their parents unless they are specifically seeking their guidance or wisdom. All members of the A.C.E.S. triad should err on the side of privacy for now. Inappropriate disclosures are the very sorts of boundary violations that contribute to family stagnation and the development of A.C.E.S. More of the same will only serve to undermine A.C.E.S. recovery.

Number four: **RESPECT EACH OTHER'S PERSONAL SPACE.** Parents of small children should feel free to enter their bedrooms without permission. If they are concerned their children are up to some sort of mischief, they should investigate their suspicions even if that means they need to "snoop" around their children's personal space. Protecting one's children from dangerous or otherwise harmful behavior is the job of a conscientious parent, *until the child becomes an adult!* From that point onward, if parents of an adult-child agree to let their child live under their roof, the parents must agree to respect their adult-child's personal space. If they cannot or will not submit to this reasonable boundary, the adult-child needs to leave the home at once. Going through the personal belongings of another adult (whether he is in your home or not) is the height of disrespect. It is a betrayal of trust. It is a gross intrusion that cannot be tolerated.

In the same way, adult-children must respect the personal space of their parents. They should never enter their parents' room uninvited.

Parents should never open the mail of their adult-child. Likewise, adult-children should never open their parents' mail.

Cell phones are private property. Reviewing another person's text messages or voicemails are violations of interpersonal boundaries. Similarly, monitoring another's Internet usage is also a violation of interpersonal boundaries. Even if you are paying the bill for your adult-child's cell phone or are paying for the Internet connection in your home that he uses, you are not entitled to intrude upon your adult-child's privacy. Stop paying the cell phone or Internet bills if doing so is causing you to feel justified in knowing the details of your adult-child's private affairs.

A.C.E.S. family members need to know the difference between what does and does not concern them.

Number five: **IDENTIFY, AGREE TO, AND ENFORCE HOUSEHOLD RULES.** A.C.E.S. parents have the right to be comfortable in their own homes. Their house, their rules. For example, if A.C.E.S. spouses are uncomfortable with the overnight guests of their adult-children, they should forbid overnight guests. Adult-children will soon be in positions to identify their own house rules but, for the time being, they will have to submit to the house rules of the people who own the houses!

Take some time to identify some reasonable house rules and put them in the contract.

STEP 6: *Adult-child independently identifies the options for his/her new living situation.*

Step six is fairly easy to tackle because it is a practical step that is measurable and concrete. It calls for the adult-child to independently identify the options for his/her new living situation.

Fortunately, with the help of the Internet, one can find ads for all kinds of housing options on dozens of websites within minutes. Although adult-children are pros at coming up with creative reasons why they cannot do something, not knowing how to use the Internet couldn't possibly be one of them. I have yet to meet anyone under the age of 35 who isn't intimately knowledgeable about how to use the Internet.

Adult-children should start by making a list of different living arrangements and then prioritize that list from most to least desirable. On that list will probably be apartments broken down by size, price, and location, rooms in private homes, apartment shares (i.e., roommates), etc. Initially, adult-children may be forced to opt for less desirable living situations in order to support themselves financially. After having private rooms all their lives, sharing rooms and/or bathrooms with strangers may be difficult for many adult-children. But right now their goal is *independent living*. It may be a long time before some adult-children will be able to achieve a comparable lifestyle to the ones they had when they lived with their parents.

One thing an adult-child should do as soon as he's identified his new living situation is to identify a contingency living situation in case his plan falls through. His back-up plan should not be to live in your house for another six months. He must identify a plan that will allow him to move out even if it's not to a permanent place. For example, he might arrange an agreement with a friend who would be able to rent him a room for a couple of months. If back-up plans, such as the aforementioned example fall through, he should research weekly rates at motels so he will have some place to go when it's time to move out.

> **STEP 7: Adult-child must understand his need to increase his income in order to live on his own and then set out to do just that.**

Your adult-child should learn what it actually costs to support himself. He will need time to ascertain how many expenses he will have when he's on his own and he will need to begin saving money (lots of it) in preparation for the launch. You may choose to be a source of information about the cost of independent living but only if your adult-child seeks you out for the information. Parents are to abstain from offering advice or unsolicited information (*see step five in this chapter*). You could say something simple like, *"Let me know if you need any help creating a budget. It's easy to overlook some monthly expenses."* If he takes you up on your offer, fine. But don't say things like, "Don't forget about electricity" or "You're going to need more than $100 a month for groceries". He will figure these things out on his own. Or he won't. Either way, he'll have the opportunity to learn, either before or after the fact.

Once your adult-child learns the reality of what things actually cost, earning enough money to maintain his current standard of living may seem like an overwhelming task, particularly if he has lived a relatively luxurious lifestyle with his parents (e.g., cable TV, Internet access, air conditioning, his own room, his own bathroom, food in the fridge). It will be your adult-child's job to relentlessly pursue earning the money he will need to live on his own. It is unlikely that adult-children who have been unemployed or underemployed for years will immediately be able to replicate the standard of living to which they are accustomed. Your adult-child may have to share a room temporarily, live in a poorer section of town than he would like, do without cable TV, Internet service, a home phone, or even air conditioning. He may have to cook inexpensive food and eat it at home instead of eating out at restaurants. He may have to shop at discount stores for groceries instead of buying specialty food items at trendy organic markets.

Chances are this sort of major lifestyle change will not be easy for most adult-children. A.C.E.S. parents would do well to brace themselves for crying, begging, promises to change, and the like from their adult-children.   A.C.E.S. parents must also brace themselves for their own feelings about having their adult-child live in conditions that they consider sub-standard. Remember, unless your adult-child is truly devoid of any personal pride, she will probably be motivated to provide more for herself in time. The goal is for her to develop into a responsible, productive adult. That doesn't happen overnight and all concerned parties should understand and accept that.

In most cases, in order to accumulate the funds necessary to move into decent (not luxurious) living situations, adult-children will probably need to find higher paying jobs than the ones they currently hold. Or they may need to subsidize their current incomes with second (or third) part-time jobs in order to accrue sufficient funds.

Your adult-child may seek your assistance in finding a job. You should feel free to point him in the right direction. It would be appropriate for your adult-child to seek your wisdom regarding employment. However, it is important that you use *Socratic Questioning* in order to help him identify the answers to his own questions. If you are unfamiliar with Socratic Questioning as a technique used to provoke critical thinking, you should look it up and study it. You will be amazed as to how useful this technique is when dealing with your adult-child. In the meantime, review the following example of Socratic Questioning in a dialogue between an adult-child and his father:

Adult-child: "Dad, will you help me find a job?"

Dad: "What kind of help do you think you need?"

Adult-child: "Well, can you call some of your friends and see if they have any openings in their companies?"

Dad: "How would that be helpful to you?"

Adult-child: "You can put in a good word for me."

Dad: "If you were going to put in a good word for yourself, what would you say?"

Adult-child: "Dad, it's who you know. You could get me in there if you say I'm your son."

Dad: "You may be right about it being "who you know". Feel free to mention that I am your dad if you decide to call them."

Adult-child: "Oh never mind. Just forget it. I don't need your help."

EXACTLY!! In this exchange, you would have helped your adult-child without enabling helplessness by coming up with all the answers to his questions. You would have empowered him think for himself by showing him you don't see it as your role to do the thinking or acting for him.

Although A.C.E.S. parents may be very tempted to do so (particularly when they see their adult-children making real efforts to earn and save money for the purpose of moving out), parents should not give their adult-children money for any reason during this time period. Responsible adult behavior should be expected and required from the very beginning of the A.C.E.S. recovery process. Receiving money without having earned it creates a sense of entitlement. It is a causal factor in the development of A.C.E.S. You may feel your adult-child should be rewarded for her earnest dedication to the A.C.E.S. recovery process. But a monetary reward will take you in the opposite direction of where the family needs to go. It would be far better for you to offer encouragement and words that reflect your confidence in your adult-child's ability to provide for herself than to 'gift' her with money.

> ***STEP 8: During the preparation for launch period, adult-child will have strict household rules he or she must adhere to in order to avoid defaulting on the contract.***

Step eight is actually a component of step five's section on *Personal Boundaries*. It requires the identification of household rules that the adult-child must adhere to in order to avoid defaulting on the launching contract. If the adult-child fails to honor the rules of the household, the launch date should be advanced, per the judgment of the parents, whether the adult-child is fully prepared or not.

While it is important to treat the adult-child like the adult that she is, the house in which she lives still belongs to you, the A.C.E.S. parents. Therefore, you are perfectly entitled to identify and enforce household rules that will make you comfortable in your own home. For example, if you are not comfortable with your son or daughter coming home after a certain hour for whatever reason, you are entitled to assign a reasonable curfew. But I want to caution A.C.E.S. parents on this subject. If you have always allowed your adult-child to come and go as she pleases, it's not terribly realistic to insist that she be home by 9 PM. In other words, if it truly does *not* bother you and you have not had a particular issue with her comings and goings in the past, the curfew thing should not be used as tool to manipulate her behavior. On the other hand, if you have made it clear all along that you do not want her coming in after a certain hour, you certainly should not put up with it during the preparation for launch phase of A.C.E.S. recovery.   Your adult-daughter, because of her inflated sense of entitlement, has not felt compelled to respect your wishes. Since she has never suffered any meaningful consequences for coming in late and disturbing you, she is most likely to continue doing so unless you are willing to strictly enforce your own household rules. Remember, your adult-child is graciously being allowed to live in your home rent-free in order for her to prepare to be launched into the world of personal responsibility. Being given ample time to prepare for this major life change should be recognized as a gift. It should not be taken for granted. For that reason, you should enforce whatever rules you feel are appropriate and reasonable.

The following is a list of some common household rules many A.C.E.S. parents have identified:

1. No overnight guests;
2. No coming in after midnight (or another time depending on the parents);
3. Must keep common house space neat and clean;
4. No alcohol or drugs in the house;
5. Must not enter the home if intoxicated; and
6. Must not use foul language in the home or speak disrespectfully to parents.

You get the idea. Be sensible when identifying the rules. Don't come up with pointless rules just for the sake of having them! Identify ones that will make you comfortable in your own home.

STEP 9: A.C.E.S. marital-units continue to strengthen their relationships via de-triangulation of their adult-children.

In step nine of the A.C.E.S. recovery process, spouses will continue to strengthen their marriages via de-triangulation of their adult-children from their marital relationships.

"De-triangulation" was discussed at length in Chapter 4 of Part I. You will recall that triangulation is a mere symptom of the overall marital malaise within the family-system. It is important for couples not to give into temptation to include their adult-children in private marital matters. As a matter of fact, it would be wise for spouses to refrain from communicating with each other through their adult-children even on the most benign matters. For example, rather than telling her adult son to let his father know that she is working late and won't be home for dinner, this A.C.E.S. spouse should call her husband directly to communicate her scheduling issues. Doing this would accomplish a couple things. First, the mother/wife would be demonstrating considerate behavior by letting her husband know where and what she will be doing after she is normally expected to be home. Second, she would not obligate her adult-son to communicate her message and would therefore avoid a potential miscommunication.

De-triangulation of the adult-child also means that she will not be leaned on for emotional support at all during the preparation for launch. The adult-child needs to focus her attention on moving out and establishing herself as a responsible adult. She should absolutely not be burdened with the emotional struggles of her parents. For example, an A.C.E.S. mother may be having a difficult time with the reality that her daughter will be moving out of the family home. While she understands and accepts that it is the right thing to do for all concerned, she may still be feeling a measure of anxiety about how her own life will change once she and her husband are alone in the home. She may need to process her feelings with another person in order to come to terms with what is happening. However, her adult-daughter is not the person she should be talking to about it! The last thing the adult-child in this scenario needs is guilty feelings about leaving "poor Mom" all alone! Poor Mom has a husband and he is the one who should be supporting his wife through this emotionally difficult time.

Utilizing aspects of pre-marital counseling, which we will explore in Chapter 3 Part II, couples will build relationships that are not dependent on third parties to minimize tension. In other words, couples will learn to tolerate and *cultivate* intimacy in their marriages.

STEP 10: Renovation plans should be made for the room that will become vacant when the adult-child moves out.

Step 10 may seem cold-hearted but it really isn't. This step involves transitioning the space occupied by the adult-child into a space that will be most useful to the people who remain in the home – namely the spouses. It is VERY important for the adult-child to understand that A.C.E.S. recovery is not a *start-n-stop* process that the family can try for a while, and if it doesn't work, go back to the way things were. The goal in A.C.E.S. recovery is NOT to go back to the way things were – ever!

Prior to A.C.E.S. recovery, the entire family lived in very unhealthy conditions. The entire family must recognize that fact and refuse to consider returning to that way of life. Therefore, the adult-child must not be allowed to assume that she can move back in if living on her own does not work out to her satisfaction. And certainly, A.C.E.S. parents must not facilitate an incorrect assumption by keeping the adult-child's bedroom intact after she is launched. In simpler terms, the room the adult-child occupied should become new space that symbolizes a measurable change in the status quo. The room should not be waiting for her if she is not able to make it in the adult world. She *has* to make it!

Planning for the new space should be a fun project for the marital-unit in an A.C.E.S. family. The couple should explore all kinds of possibilities for the new space with each partner making his or her wish list for how the room will be used. The room could be used as a retreat for meditation, prayer, or quiet reflection. Maybe you will decide to make it a library. It could become a crafts or hobby room. Maybe it could even become a home gym. It's up to the couple to decide how the space will be used but every effort should be made to remake the room so that it could not be mistaken for the room once occupied by the adult-child.

Psychologically, this may be a painful step for both the parents and the adult-child. After all, the adult-child is not dead! It may seem as if the goal is to hide any evidence of his existence after the launch. Not so. The goal is only to clearly transmit the message that real change is taking place. Again, there should be no visible bridge back to dysfunction. An adult-child's unchanged bedroom is just that: a visible bridge.

One of the hardest parts of converting the room will be the packing up. It is amazing how much an adult-child can cram into a single room! But the proactive packing up of all items that are not required for day-to-day functioning is an important part of step 10. Things that should be packed up a month or two before the launch date might include photo albums, books, personal décor, mementos, and clothes that are not currently seasonal. Basically, things you would not pack to go on a two-week vacation should be stored until the launch. Doing this will reinforce the reality of the adult-child's imminent transition into his own home.

Even more important is that the process of packing will help family members psychologically adjust to the coming launch while the adult-child is *still in the home.* Family members will be able to see the room transforming into a new space little by little. Go ahead and do some preliminary measurements of the room and perhaps start purchasing the things you will need for renovation. If these actions are taken in advance, the renovation can begin immediately after the launch.

STEP 11: A.C.E.S. parents and their adult-child should begin celebrating the upcoming launch by taking stock of the progress they've made over the last several months.

Step 11 encourages A.C.E.S. parents and their adult-child to begin celebrating the upcoming launch by taking stock of the progress they've made over the last several months. "Launch Day" is a truly momentous occasion and should be recognized as such. Therefore, A.C.E.S. families should make every effort to reflect on how far they've come as family-units and as individuals throughout the A.C.E.S. recovery process.

As a part of step 11, I often encourage each member of the A.C.E.S. triad to generate letters to the other two members of the triad so they can pensively express their thoughts about the recovery process. Hopefully, the reflections contained within each letter will express admiration, gratitude, and even sorrow for the pain they caused to one another prior to A.C.E.S. recovery. Once the letters are exchanged, it might be nice to have a celebratory dinner or something of the like. The act of completing step 11 will help the triad to maintain familial harmony in spite of the impending launch. A.C.E.S. recovery does not interrupt family members' love for one another. It simply prompts a necessary change in the way the family functions.

> *STEP 12: The 12th and final step in the launching process requires that the adult-child develop a written contingency plan if his attempt at independence begins to fail.*

The 12th and final step in the launching process requires that the adult-child develop a written contingency plan if his attempt at independence begins to fail. Put simply, the adult-child must come up with a few back-up plans he can use on a temporary basis if he needs to re-group and find another permanent living arrangement. While solid preparation for the launch will help prevent the likelihood of a major set-back, unforeseen problems can arise. If and when this happens, the adult-child must have a plan to solve his problem that would not include a move back into the family home. *Note: Step 12 is distinct from step six in that step 12 calls for the development of a variety of contingency plans to be used when/if a particular emergency occurs* after *the launch has taken place, whereas step six calls for the identification of a contingency plan that would still allow the adult-child to move out if her original move-out-plan was to fall through.*

In order to avoid a Mayday call that could potentially put A.C.E.S. parents on the spot to rescue their adult-child, it would be a good idea to inform the parents exactly what the contingency plan is. A.C.E.S. parents will feel more secure if their adult-child already has a plan to deal with emergencies, should they arise. I will give you an example of a simple contingency plan at the end of this section.

An adult-child might need to utilize her contingency plan for a sudden and significant change in living costs. For example, if your adult-child's roommate decides to take a job out of town and gives your daughter only 30 days notice to find a new roommate, it could become a big problem. Most adult-children will be living on a budget for the first time in their lives when they start living on their own and it's likely that the budget will be pretty tight for a while. If your adult-child experiences a sudden and significant change in her living costs, she will understand why it was so important for her to have a sizeable prudent reserve of funds before she moved out of your home.

Referencing the above example, during the time it takes to find a suitable roommate, the adult-child may need to draw on her savings to stay afloat. Ideally, however, it would be better to have actual people in mind to fill the vacancy such as a cousin, another adult-child stuck at home, or even the friend of a friend. In a circumstance like this, the adult-child ought to be very aggressive in her attempt to find a new roommate. In other words, there should be no delay in finding another person to fill the occupancy. If the adult-child is unable to find a person quickly, she should be prepared to post the vacancy on bulletin boards or with roommate finding services. She should not rest until she solves the problem of finding a roommate.

However, if despite her BEST efforts, she still cannot find a roommate, she may need to move into another living arrangement herself. She should know who would be in a position to put her up in an emergency. And she should be willing to pay whoever she lives with up to the same amount of rent she was paying before moving out of her place. Sleeping on someone's couch for a couple of months, after having a place of her own, could be rough *(especially if she would be spending nearly the same amount of money she paid to have her own place)*. Chances are she will be very motivated to identify a way to get back into a permanent living arrangement as soon as possible!

A.C.E.S. parents may be tempted to formulate their adult-child's contingency plan for him, not fully trusting his resourcefulness in a crisis. This would be a mistake. The parents need to let their adult-child figure out how to take care of himself regardless of what comes up unexpectedly.

Hopefully, the contingency plan will not be needed, at least not right away. But in any case, as long as he has a contingency plan already in place, the adult-child won't be caught like a deer in the headlights if something does come up.

Once step 12 has been completed, the adult-child will be launched into the world as a self-supporting adult. The moving day will officially mark the end of the concrete aspect of A.C.E.S. recovery. It will also mark the beginning of the critical, but more abstract, parts of the A.C.E.S. recovery program.

As promised, below you will find an example of a well-conceived contingency plan:

- *If my roommate suddenly moves out*: I have a list of roommate agencies that would be able to find me a roommate in less than a week so I wouldn't get stuck paying all the rent while I looked for a roommate by myself.
- *If I lose my job*: I plan to immediately file for unemployment and start looking for another job the same day. I have a list of companies that do the same thing as I'm doing now so I could apply to those companies and be able to offer my experience along with current knowledge of the industry. This would likely increase my chances of quickly replacing my job whereas if I tried to find a job in an industry where I have no experience, it might take considerably longer to replace my income. My resume is saved on my computer so all I'd have to do is update it and submit it. I have a list of people I can network with who might be in a position to help me find a suitable job. I will periodically check in with those people to keep those contacts current.
- *If something happens to my car:* I have learned about how to get to my job on the bus. I also found out that the local community college fixes cars for free in their auto mechanics department. I could also offer a coworker gas money if he or she can help me get to and from work until I get my car fixed.
- *If I get hurt or become ill*: I will investigate my eligibility for temporary disability benefits immediately and/or draw upon my emergency savings as modestly as I can until I am well.

Chapter 2 – Phase 2: Reorganization of the A.C.E.S. – free Family

Once the launching of your adult-child has taken place, you might assume that the *important* part of the A.C.E.S. recovery process is done and that the rest of the process is just "extra" work you don't really need to complete. I urge you to recognize that relapse, at least to some degree, is likely unless the family is willing to complete the recovery process in its entirety. A critical part of the A.C.E.S. recovery process is to reorganize the family structure with each member assuming his or her proper role within the family-unit.

Clearly, in A.C.E.S. families, family roles become distorted over time. Members of typical A.C.E.S. families come to abandon their appropriate roles within their family-units in order to accommodate the perpetuation of dysfunctional family relationships. In reviewing the various ways family members function throughout the course of active A.C.E.S., it is plain to see that adult-children were routinely placed in parental roles. Parents assumed the roles of children, marital-partners interacted like rivaling siblings, and adult-children were infantilized. Fortunately, with much conscious effort, A.C.E.S. families are capable of re-establishing appropriate family roles (and will need to do so to avoid a family relapse).

The Patriarch

Naturally, fathers should be *patriarchs* within their family-units. A patriarch, in the general sense of the word, is a man who is the head of a family or group. He is respected and experienced and most often is the senior male figure in a family.

A.C.E.S. fathers, as a rule, surrender their patriarchal roles when they tolerate and foster disrespect. They do this when they allow their adult-children to disregard their advice, instructions, and commands in order to maintain the dysfunctional status quo. Likewise, A.C.E.S. husbands do this when they refuse to be partners to their wives. Instead, A.C.E.S. husbands regularly allow their adult-children to supply their wives with the emotional support that they should be providing.

A.C.E.S. fathers/husbands may have behaved badly for decades. Their less than admirable behavior probably led their wives and children to justify their disrespect for them. It was immaturity, among other things, that caused many of these men to engage in extra-marital affairs, addictions, or otherwise juvenile behaviors. And in the process, these gentlemen yielded their patriarchal dignity.

But once they are able to recognize the ways in which they willfully surrendered their rightful places in their families, A.C.E.S. fathers/husbands can begin repairing the damage. To start off with, patriarchs should make direct amends to their family members. For starters, they can begin the process of making amends by claiming and adopting their patriarchal roles. Patriarchs do this by expecting and insisting upon respectful treatment from their adult-children and their wives.

As their reputations for being immature pushovers or overbearing brutes have been reinforced for decades, the reestablishment of their proper patriarchal roles will take some time and can only be accomplished by setting *consistent* limits, living dignified lives, and leading by example. They will have to enforce reasonable consequences for disrespectful behavior, which will probably be difficult to do because they may not feel entitled to being treated respectfully due to their past mistakes. But if the family is to recover from A.C.E.S. everyone, including the rightful patriarch, must submit to some discomfort in favor of overall family wellness.

Before proceeding, let me offer an example of a limit a patriarch might set with his adult-child. Let's say an adult-child chides his father for not remembering his (the adult-child's) mother's birthday. The father, whether his adult-son is right or wrong, ought to terminate the conversation with his son, saying something like, "It is not your place to judge or admonish me for something that is between your mother and me. The matter is none of your concern and we will not discuss it any further." Were the father to *defend* his forgetfulness to his adult-son, he would be acting the role of a child being reprimanded. The patriarch would be allowing his son to take a parental stance, thereby assuming the patriarch's role in the interaction.

Now, in all fairness to those family members who were hurt by them, it would not be appropriate for A.C.E.S. fathers/husbands to simply disregard their past behaviors as though they had never happened. They can't exploit their new found roles as patriarchs by wielding their power like dictators. Their past mistakes must be acknowledged, as it generally garners respect when people admit and take responsibility for the wrongs they have done. Therefore, it would be wise for patriarchs to have conversations with their families that opened with statements such as the following: "I realize that I have not always behaved in a way that commanded your respect. In fact, I have behaved very badly at times and I regret that fact very much. It's true that my failures to lead this family properly have caused you to see me in an unfavorable light, which I understand and for which I do not fault you. However, I have come to realize that it is never too late to change course and I am committed to a new way of living which will require me to serve as the head of this family. Some of you may struggle with the new way we are going to interact but I am committed to being the patriarch this family needs once and for all. I hope you will forgive my past mistakes. I don't intend to make them again."

Fathers must be willing to sacrifice what may have been peer-like relationships with their children in order to assume their rightful roles in their family-systems. Fathers should necessarily be sources of wisdom. However, they must abstain from imposing their opinions and suggestions on their adult-children unless their adult-children are specifically soliciting their advice.

Fathers should be firm, kind, and serious when setting limits and boundaries with their adult-children. They should implement changes to existing family norms rationally and without a lot of emotional expression. They should strive to present components of the new regime calmly and deliberately, emphasizing the goal of refining the present circumstances for the overall good of their families.

Finally, A.C.E.S. husbands should strive to be the supportive, comforting, intimate partners their wives have always needed. They should embrace their roles as 'partners' within their marital relationships and refuse to be "mothered" or parentified by their wives. They should take care of themselves in ways that let their wives know that they are not children who need to be reminded to bring a jacket when it's cold outside, for example. However, they are to always be respectful of their wives' intentions to be helpful and always consider their input with kindly esteem. They collaborate with their wives on important matters; they do not dominate *or* allow themselves to be browbeaten.

Patriarchs are the principal representatives of their marital-units, '*Executives*' who cherish and respect their wives. Patriarchs deeply value the wisdom of their wives and routinely rely upon it when crafting family policies.

The Matriarch

A.C.E.S. mothers/wives should be *matriarchs*. While a patriarch's role is to *enforce* the changes in a restructured family-system, the matriarch's role should involve supporting the patriarch by lovingly communicating the necessity and appropriateness of reorganizing the family to all parties involved.

A.C.E.S. women who have lost respect for their husbands over the decades (because of their husbands' lack of appropriate leadership in their families) may have a hard time letting go of authoritarian roles. This is particularly true if they have always played the dominant parental figure in their family-systems. They may not trust their husbands to lead their families in responsible ways. They may have undermined their husbands' authority over the years by openly "trumping" him on certain decisions. (*Note: On the other hand, A.C.E.S. women whose rightful family positions were overshadowed by overbearing husbands may struggle to assume more authoritative roles*).

False pride may inhibit the ability of many A.C.E.S. mothers/wives to submit to the A.C.E.S. recovery process as a whole. The key word in the previous sentence is "false". *Genuine* pride enables one to assume one's proper role in a family. Mothers/wives ought to feel a sense of genuine pride in their roles as family matriarchs.

Foremost in assuming the role of the family matriarch is being able to support the family patriarch as the head of the family. Women may feel that letting go of an authoritarian role in order to assume a supportive role would represent a dramatic downshift in power within their family-systems. Let me clarify that what these women would be "supporting" is their husbands' patriarchal role in their families. That's all. Supporting their husbands in being the heads of their families does not mean that the matriarchs will lose their voices in the household.

In the spirit of achieving A.C.E.S. recovery, I'm asking A.C.E.S. matriarchs to allow their husbands to become front-men in their marital-units, the designated heads of their families. Please understand that you being supportive of your husband does not mean that you will be surrendering spousal equality in your marriage. It only means that you will allow your husband to *represent* your marital-unit to the rest of your family members so you can, together, present a united front to all. *(For matriarchs that still find themselves resistant to their husbands being the sole head of their families, think of this: If your husband is the head of your family and you are supporting him, then you must be the neck of the family! Everyone knows that the neck turns the head!)*

As said in the previous section, men must step into their proper roles as patriarchs in their families in order for A.C.E.S. recovery to take place. Part of the matriarch's role is to help facilitate the establishment of her husband's patriarchy. That is easier done than said. That's not a misprint: it is easier *done* than *said*.

Of course, when I direct A.C.E.S. women to become true matriarchs by allowing their husbands to emerge as leaders in their families, they usually have plenty of objections. However, when they *actually take my counsel*, most A.C.E.S. women report feelings of relief and satisfaction. The satisfaction they feel comes from 1) uniting with their husbands and, 2) freeing themselves of the conviction that they have to be all things to all people, including leader, decision-maker, policy-setter, disciplinarian, nurse, and lover.

Some cultures recognize the matriarch as the supreme leader of the family. That is to say that her authority trumps that of any man in the family. I want to be clear about the way I am defining the proper role of the matriarch in the recovering A.C.E.S. family. I adopt a more generalized concept of the *matriarch* as a woman who is highly respected by her family and to whom the family turns for guidance and wisdom.

While the matriarch certainly holds a position of dominance, authority, and respect in the family, the thing that distinguishes her from the patriarch is that her dominance, authority and respect are, above all, *feminine*. She is the perfect complement to her husband's masculine dominance which should be focused on concrete matters that are logistical in nature. Patriarchs are responsible for indoctrinating family members with wholesome family principles. In contrast, a matriarch's authority essentially resides in the realm of the abstract, dealing mostly with matters of the heart. She is the *feelings* expert.

True matriarchs don't shy away from or *resent* their feminine strengths. They never try to hide or repress their strengths, or seek to demonstrate less natural qualities (i.e., masculine qualities) in order to maintain powerful positions in their families. A matriarch's power is a different (but equivalent) kind of power.

Matriarchs nurture and empower. They exemplify dignity and grace. They possess an abundance of wisdom and strength. They practice loving detachment from overly dependent children, grandchildren, and husbands. They allow their loved ones to accumulate their own wisdom via their mistakes, understanding that wisdom is most often born of pain. They provide guidance only when it is sought. They sift through the content of their loved ones' troubles, easily identifying true feelings and emotions. They are careful not to solve problems or rescue able-individuals. They support their husbands publically and consult with them privately. Their authority is beyond question, brandished with tenderness.

Matriarchs should redirect attempts to be used as intermediaries between A.C.E.S. fathers and adult-children. Above all, they should refuse to allow their marriages to be compromised by advocating for their adult-children who may think new family policies are too harsh.

The Marital-unit

Obviously, it is critical for marital-partners to be united in decisions pertaining to the reorganization of their family-systems. Husbands and wives must support one another in their reestablished roles, offering reassurance and gratitude for each other's willingness to meaningfully participate in each component of the reorganization process, particularly when it comes to adopting the roles of patriarch and matriarch in their family-systems.

Adult-children

Adult-children, through no fault of their own, were triangulated into their parents' marriages and were enlisted to play roles as parents, spouses, and finally, infantile adult-children who were to become increasingly dependent over time. Be that as it may, as adult-children recovering from A.C.E.S., they now need to assume adult roles within their families of origin.

Practicing self-reliance is part of being an adult. When it comes to making simple decisions, adults should be able to rely upon their own judgment and common sense. Sometimes our common sense dictates that we should seek advice when charting unfamiliar territory. It is smart to seek advice when one doesn't know what one is doing! But adult-children are often very confused when it comes to knowing when and why they should seek counsel. They are likewise confused about whom to seek counsel from.

When living at home, adult-children usually have things backwards when it comes to seeking counsel. For example, when an adult-child manages to accumulate a significant sum of money, she may consult a friend about how to spend it and may end up with a new pair of ski boots. That same adult-child may go to her *mother* to ask whether she should confront her boyfriend about text- messaging his old girlfriend. Huh? Given the two issues, this adult-child has her *counselors* mixed up. She's going to her friend for financial counsel and her mother for romantic advice. Obviously, when making financial decisions, it would be wise to seek counsel from someone who actually has some money and experience in managing finances. And when discussing a peer-related matter, such as a romantic issue, it would make sense to seek guidance from a peer who could relate to the problem.

If my adult-daughter came to me with the text-messaging issue, I'd just tell her to dump the guy she's dating because she obviously doesn't trust him. I wouldn't be able to get my head around the dilemma at all. The solution would be too apparent to me. A girlfriend, however, would be far more understanding and obliging in helping my kid negotiate the waters of a technological love affair.

On the other hand, if my adult-daughter had come to me with the financial question, I certainly would not have advised her to buy ski boots! I would have encouraged her to save the money for upcoming expenses (e.g., car registration, text books, bills, etc.) and to put a portion of the money away for a rainy day.

A.C.E.S. adult-children and their parents are all mixed up in terms of what they should and should not discuss with one another. As in the previous example, A.C.E.S. adult-children routinely over-disclose personal problems (such as romantic troubles) and under-disclose practical matters (such as finances).

Adult-children should have practiced making personal decisions without the counsel of their parents during the preparation for launch process (*see the Interpersonal Boundaries section in Part II, Chapter 1, Step 5*). Adult-children cannot assume their proper roles as independent and self-respecting members of their families of origin unless they can keep the personal details of their lives from their parents. *(Note to adult-children: Trust me, your parents don't need and shouldn't want to know about every aspect of your love life, your social life, or your daily routine. That's what friends are for. If you don't have any, get some. You will never unburden yourself from the roles of quasi-parent and surrogate-spouse to your parent(s) unless you become a fully-functioning, self-contained adult.)*

When I instruct adult-children to keep their personal lives private from their parents, they say things like, "But my mom is my best friend, I tell her everything" or "My dad already knows everything about my life, we tell each other our problems all the time" and "My mom wants to know everything about my life…she will go crazy if I just cut her off." When adult-children neglect peer relationships in favor of relating to one or both of their parents as peers, triangulation is perpetuated. Establishing proper family roles, a critical component of A.C.E.S. recovery, is impossible if family members are still triangulating one another.

It can be very difficult for an adult-child to establish herself as an adult in a family that has always regarded her as somewhat inept when it comes to running her own life. If any given A.C.E.S. adult-child is honest with herself however, she will readily agree that she has made some pretty poor decisions prior to submitting to the A.C.E.S. recovery process. And, quite frankly, it is probable that she has become comfortable in the role of the 'screw-up' as it has allowed her to behave irresponsibly with little consequence.

For A.C.E.S. recovery to be successful, adult-children must begin conducting their lives in responsible, dignified ways. They must recognize and accept that they are underdeveloped in practical and emotional matters and need to catch up to their age-appropriate levels of functioning. Fortunately, living independently will allow them to catch up very quickly!

Once they have been launched, adult-children should understand that it is not acceptable to behave like college students who are away at school but who are still dependent on their parents financially and otherwise. For example, adult-children should not bring their laundry to their parents' house, as so many college students do when they are home on vacation from school. They should not drop in for dinner without being invited. They should not raid the cupboards and refrigerators when they visit, treating their parents' kitchens like grocery stores. An adult-child should not be on his parents' car-insurance policy as an additional driver. He should not be on his parents' cell phone *family-plan*. An adult-child should not have keys to her parents' house, allowing her to come and go as though she lived there. If it is decided that an adult-child will have a key to his parents' home, the circumstances for its use should be made very clear (e.g., emergencies, to water plants or feed pets when the marital-unit is away from home, etc.).

Adult-children should accept, embrace and REJOICE in the establishment of appropriate family roles. They are the greatest beneficiaries of the new regime. Their challenge will be to accept the necessary behavioral changes their parents are making in order to recover from A.C.E.S. They may, at times, feel shut out, unwelcome, neglected, lonely, angry, or jealous. And given the way the family has always interacted, adult-children may actually experience feelings of displacement in the world. This is both normal and temporary. A.C.E.S. adult-children would be wise to anticipate some of these feelings, as they are likely to emerge occasionally. It is not necessary for adult-children to be blindsided with feelings of rejection, etc. Knowing what to expect will help adult-children cope when unhappy feelings surface.

The Family as a Whole

The adult-child's move out of the family home dissembles the original A.C.E.S. family-unit, allowing family members to form separate, independently functioning family-systems. In the new model, the marital-unit will resume *"couplehood"* after an extra-long period of active parenting. The spouses will no longer exist as a marital-unit in the former A.C.E.S. family-system. They will form a self-contained family-unit made up of a husband and a wife. The adult-child will shed his role as the dependent adult-child in the pre-existing family-system, becoming an independent family-unit. That is to say, the adult-child will establish his life as a single-adult who is free to institute his own norms and ways of being in the world, which may or may not resemble the ways of his family of origin. Each family-unit should be mutually respected without attempts to impose its own practices on the other.

It would be prudent for all family members to be watchful with regard to maintaining the reorganization of their families. Old behavioral patterns will be very easy to slip back into unless all family members maintain their commitments to the A.C.E.S. recovery program.

One thing I suggest to all family members is for each of them to keep a running list of all the good things A.C.E.S. recovery is bringing to their lives. I also ask them to keep a list of all the negative things A.C.E.S. did to their families and to their inter-familial relationships prior to recovery. Finally, I ask them to identify all the positive aspects of their newly established family roles. And when the going gets tough, I encourage them to review those lists again and again and again. Eventually, their new (appropriate) family roles will take root, providing the fruits of healthy family relationships.

Chapter 3 – Phase 3: Renovate Your Marriage *during* the A.C.E.S. Remission Process and Beyond

Couples should not wait until the launch has taken place to address the state of their marriages. As a matter of fact, it makes sense for couples to focus much of their attention on building new foundations for happier marital relationships particularly while they are struggling to manage the emotional challenges of detaching from their adult-children. As you now know, a dysfunctional marriage is what leads to the development of A.C.E.S. Therefore, it is imperative for the marital healing process to begin as soon as possible. Spouses will still have plenty of work to do on their marriages after their adult-children have been launched but they should get started long before their adult-children actually move out.

There are five basic components required in the marital renovation process. They are as follows: 1) a review of triangulation; 2) a period of sexual abstinence; 3) a genuine courtship; 4) resolving (presumably) irreconcilable differences; and 5) completing the renovation worksheets (at the end of this chapter). Let's take them one at a time.

Triangulation

To get started, couples first need to review the concept of *triangulation* which was first introduced in Chapter 4 of Part I. In that chapter we discussed the concept of triangulation at length, as it represents the breeding ground for A.C.E.S. Needless to say, it is a critical concept to grasp when it comes to understanding the evolution of the A.C.E.S. family dilemma. Consider that "triangulation" has been referenced some 30 times in this book already! Without a doubt, understanding the mechanism of triangulation is a critical component of the A.C.E.S. recovery process.

The process of triangulation requires the recruitment of a third person (in A.C.E.S. families, this would be an adult-child) who is used to reduce marital tension. Therefore, triangulation negatively impacts all inter-familial relationships, including marital relationships in A.C.E.S. families. While triangulation can occur without A.C.E.S., A.C.E.S. cannot occur without triangulation. A couple's inability to tolerate marital intimacy drives triangulation. Therefore, achieving marital intimacy is a key facet of the A.C.E.S. recovery process. It is the stuff that paves the road to marital renovation.

In order for marital renovation to begin, it is important for spouses to understand why they were not able to achieve or maintain marital intimacy over the course of their relationships in spite of their love for one another. Couples, whose relationships facilitated the development of the A.C.E.S. family dilemma, *subconsciously sought* to avoid marital intimacy by triangulating their children into their marriages.

It is important for A.C.E.S. couples to understand that their *triangulation inclination* was not triggered by parenthood. Rather, it grew out of their premarital relationships during which they made certain mistakes which blocked their ability to develop genuinely intimate relationships.

A Period of Sexual Abstinence

Chapter 2 of Part I addressed relationship hazards that lead to the development of A.C.E.S. If your family developed A.C.E.S., Chapter 2 probably helped you recognize that at least some of the identified hazards were present in your premarital relationship. The first of the hazards Chapter 2 addressed was premarital sex. We discussed the negative impact it has on couples' ability to achieve genuine intimacy prior to marriage.

The marital renovation process is all about generating genuine marital intimacy. If our goal is to generate genuine intimacy, we must be willing to do the things that would facilitate its development. Abstaining from premarital sex is one of the things that helps facilitate emotional and spiritual intimacy *prior* to marriage. Hence, sexual abstinence during the marital renovation process is a tool we will use to build genuine intimacy. It is a critical part of the renovation process. But don't worry, sexual abstinence is a very temporary component of the marital renovation process – your sexual relationship will resume soon enough.

As you read the next few pages you might begin to wonder how the topic of premarital sex is relevant to marital renovation. Obviously, you are already married and *pre*marital *sex* is no longer a possibility. But read on; you will soon understand how the issue of premarital sex applies to your circumstances.

While some A.C.E.S. couples remained abstinent from sex prior to marriage, they are the rare exception to the rule. My work with A.C.E.S. couples has allowed me to hypothesize that in the vast majority of cases, premarital sex (among other things) piloted the development and exacerbation of marital intimacy problems. And, as we have learned, a lack of marital intimacy is a determinant factor in the development of A.C.E.S. *(see Chapter 1, Part I).*

I am sympathetic towards spouses who were not properly informed about the psychological and emotional risks of sex before marriage. Had they received information about the potential ramifications of premarital sex, they may have opted to wait. Of course hindsight is 20/20 and those who had sex before marriage (without any understanding of how premarital sex could affect their future relationships and personal psyches) should not berate themselves about it now. When we know better we typically do better.

While this book is certainly not intended to be a moral teaching, we can glean a fair amount of sensible guidance from religious/moral sources when it comes to the rationale supporting sexual abstinence prior to marriage. Per religious sensibility, sex is a *privilege* of marriage. It is the physical expression of our wedding vows in which we give ourselves completely to our spouses. Our sexuality is the most personal aspect of our physical beings and ought to be reserved for the person with whom we choose to spend our lives. In the confines of a loving marriage, sex brings partners closer together and it renews marital commitments. On the other hand, loveless sex (i.e., without a commitment) takes a toll on self-esteem, diminishes one's capacity for intimacy, impacts one's ability to enjoy sex in the future, and compromises one's ability to maintain emotional sensitivity when it comes to sexuality. Additionally, premarital sex can be very confusing (i.e., mixed message) for some partners. For example, it is not uncommon for one or both partners to interpret sex as confirmation of devoted love when it is merely confirmation of physical attraction. If a given premarital relationship fell apart during a period of sexual abstinence before marriage, it may be because the partners became overly reliant upon sex to *feel* close. The partners were probably unable to access that feeling of genuine closeness without sex. In other words, sex was the glue holding the couple together.

You might be surprised by the number of **un**married couples who come in for *relationship* counseling (not premarital counseling) before they are even engaged. My instinct is to tell the two well-intentioned people to RUN from the relationship. If they are having big enough problems to need counseling *PRIOR* to marriage, I want to tell them that they are almost certainly incompatible and that things are likely to get far worse once they experience the inevitable stressors of marriage. But, unless their relationship is downright abusive and destructive, I usually contain my thoughts on the matter in order to focus on *their* goal of working out their differences. Sometimes partners can work things out. Most of the time, they cannot. But they tend to marry anyway and too many end up miserable and divorced.

When I work with A.C.E.S. couples, I always take a thorough history of their sexual relationships. Interestingly, I find that their sexual relationships are much like the sexual relationships of unmarried couples that seek relationship counseling. When the unmarried couples present me with a profile of their respective sexual relationships, here is what I typically find:

1. They are currently sleeping together;
2. They had sex within the first two weeks of their relationships; many had sex the first or second time they saw each other;
3. They have very different ideas about how often they should have sex; and
4. They describe their sexual relationships as boring or meaningless.

Unmarried women, overwhelmingly, are psychologically and emotionally confused by sex *(we will address this confusion more fully later in the chapter)*. They tend to recognize premarital sex as a confirmation of love. A woman may think, "If he is having sex with me, he is committed to our relationship and wants to be with me more than any other woman." A.C.E.S. married women are also confused by sex. But different from their unmarried counterparts, they interpret sex as a confirmation of their husbands' need for physical gratification as opposed to their need to express love. Therefore, when they don't experience intimate love in other aspects of their relationships, married women tend to resent their husbands' desire for (or insistence upon) sex.

Men interpret premarital sex as confirmation of *their* importance (i.e., value) to their partners. They see sex as a relationship achievement *(we will talk more about that later in the chapter)*. That is not to say that they don't have regard for their partners but, for most men, premarital sex is not confirmation of a permanent commitment. If anything, men see premarital sex as proof of their acceptance as they are. After "achieving" premarital sex, they usually believe that they no longer have to "work" to win their partners over. In other words, "If she is having sex with me, she certainly accepts me as I am. I don't have to prove anything to her. I don't have to work hard to win her over anymore. I've already won."

Married men consider sex to be an expression of their love as well as a means to be close to their spouses when they are otherwise at odds. When a man's attempt to show love sexually is rejected, it is very painful as he sees it as a rejection of his entire self.

But let's focus on unmarried partners for a moment since they provide the seed from which intimacy-lacking marital-units stem. When unmarried partners rely on sex to make them feel close, united, committed or loved, they are headed for trouble. Having a dependency on premarital sex cheats couples out of *genuine* courtships.

A genuine courtship is the prelude to a happy marriage. It is the period of a romantic relationship when partners work to gain each other's love and trust. During this time, we are particularly attentive to each other, truly desiring to know one another intimately. We try to win favor by presenting ourselves in the best possible light. We are selfless during this period; generous, thoughtful and courteous. The courtship is one of the BEST times in a loving relationship! But so many A.C.E.S. couples never enjoyed real courtships because premarital sex got in the way. What a shame.

Consider that premarital sex can actually persuade partners to marry who are ill-suited for one another. Their sexual compatibility may block out awareness of many important *in*compatibilities in their relationship, incompatibilities that could destroy their relationship. Premarital sex may severely impair their judgment.

If premarital sex is the thing that causes partners to feel close, safe, and secure, their relationship is sure to suffer down the line when sexuality often takes a back seat to parenting, careers, and otherwise busy, hectic schedules (not to mention aging). In actuality, sex cannot overcome the kind of insecurity that exists merely because partners don't (yet) adequately know one another. Sex is simply not able to generate real feelings of security. Feelings can never be coerced. Insecurity in romantic relationships stems from a lack of spiritual and emotional closeness between the partners, not from a lack of sex. Partners become spiritually and emotionally close when they spend time together engaging in meaningful discussions, sharing meaningful occasions, and bonding via meaningful pursuits.

Insecurity means *not* feeling secure. Security is another word for safety. We feel safe around people we trust. We tend to trust people we know well. Do you really trust people you don't know? You might trust a stranger to hold your place in line for a ride at Disneyland or something like that. But would you ever trust a stranger at Disneyland to watch your young child? Hold your wallet? Your car keys? Your house keys? No, of course not. But millions of people trust their sexual selves with total strangers as if their sexuality was devoid of any value whatsoever. We must know, *and know well,* the people we give our sexuality to or we pay a steep price. The cost is paid out in self-esteem, capacity for intimacy, ability to enjoy sex in the future, and the ability to maintain emotional sensitivity when it comes to sexuality.

Partners come to truly know one another through the sharing of their internal selves. While sex within the confines of a loving relationship can be an expression of love, it cannot produce intimacy because sex is a sharing of our *external* selves.

Some A.C.E.S. spouses, mostly those who cohabited before marriage, had sex for years before getting married. By the time they got married, many couples reported that their sexual relationships had *already* become routine! Nowadays, many unmarried partners see premarital cohabitation as a *necessary* experiment that will help them to determine whether their relationships could evolve into viable marriages. Sadly, it is often the *living-together-experiment* itself that blocks the development of viable marriages.

While the preceding pages may seem like they were written for couples who have *yet* to marry, they were actually written for you: the A.C.E.S. marital-unit. Perhaps you're thinking *"But we've been married for 30 years — it's not like we can go back in time and not have premarital sex. It's true that we had premarital sex, but what can we do about it now?"* You're right. We can't go back in time. But we can start over.

The goal of this chapter is to teach A.C.E.S. couples how to renovate their marriages. *'Renovation'* means to make new. In order for A.C.E.S. marital-units to make their marriages new, they must start with clean slates. They have to knock down the old ways of relating and implement healthy relationship strategies that are designed to foster intimacy.

I expressed my next point in Chapter 2, Part I but it bears reviewing at this juncture: *When people have sex prior to developing the level of intimacy necessary for meaningful, fulfilling marriages, their minds register the primal assumption (on a subconscious level) that they have already reached the height of spiritual and emotional closeness. Once their sexual relationship has commenced, spouses believe that it is no longer necessary for them to explore each other on internal levels. So naturally, they stop striving to get to know each other spiritually and emotionally. And as we've learned, spirituality and emotionality are the building blocks of intimate relationships (see the renovation worksheets at the end of this chapter).*

It's true that partners (especially partners who have been married for decades like most A.C.E.S. marital-units) can love each other deeply and still not be connected on an intimate level. If you are having trouble understanding how a relationship can be loving but not intimate, consider the other love-based relationships in your lives. We love our parents, siblings, etc., but we do not necessarily have intimate relationships with them. Do you share your innermost thoughts with everyone you love deeply? Do you tell your brother your most private thoughts? Do you confess your deepest fears to your dad? Your Aunt Marge? Your great Grandfather? Do you even like and enjoy all of the people you love? Think about it. Intimacy is not a requisite ingredient in all love-based relationships, but it is a critical component of a satisfying marriage. Without intimacy, marriages are extra prone to triangulation.

The marital renovation process involves the critical component of sexual abstinence until both partners feel a genuine sense of spiritual (i.e., meaningful) and emotional intimacy with one another. Working through the renovation worksheets at the end of this chapter will help spouses talk through their differences and come to know one another more deeply than ever before. You will listen to and carefully consider your partner's thoughts and feelings on various issues. You will try to see things from his or her point of view. Hopefully, you will come to understand one another and become willing to compromise or even change your own stance on various topics.

There are tried and true ways to avoid sex *before* marriage but to abstain from sex after decades of marriage may seem silly or even impossible. Logistically, sleeping apart will be difficult unless you have an extra bedroom (but most of you should have an extra bedroom if your adult-child has moved out of your home). Try to figure out a way to sleep apart, even if one of you sleeps on a couch in the living room. At some point, if the third component (a genuine courtship) of marital renovation is properly executed and includes lots of romance, fun, and sharing, you will probably begin to feel a real longing to express your love for each other in a physical way. And that would be the point at which you should resume your sexual relationship.

A Genuine Courtship

As we continue on our path of recovery, A.C.E.S. marital-units will be *starting over*, beginning with a formal courtship. And your courtship will be of the old-fashioned sort which means you will not be having sex! The length of your courtship will depend upon how rapidly you are able to achieve spiritual and emotional intimacy. Don't panic! I promise your sexual relationship will be resumed in short order. Keep reading.

When you begin your marital renovation, make a list of things you wish you had done before premarital sex terminated your courtship and allowed you to act like an *old-married couple.*

Here are some things A.C.E.S. partners have identified as things they could do to make their courtships exciting and special:

1. *Make the effort to dress up for each other* – Wear stylish, contemporary clothing that presents you in your best light. Don't walk around in sweats and dirty old jeans all the time! You are trying to *impress* the one you love.
2. *Make plans to go to new and interesting places* – Visit interesting places that prompt reflections, reactions, and feelings you can

share with each other. Go to new and exotic restaurants, try new foods, and visit different towns when you go on dates. By the way, men should try to plan some dates without their wives knowing the details. Most women appreciate it when men take the initiative to plan special dates in advance. Thoughtful planning makes women feel cherished and desired. Men can expect to receive large romantic dividends in the end when they make the effort to surprise their wives with something she'd enjoy.

3. _Join book clubs for couples_ – You can read together and discuss your thoughts and reactions to the literature. Sharing personal impressions about art and literature with our partners is an intimacy building exercise.

4. _Learn to ballroom dance (if you are so inclined)_ – This is an opportunity for couples to practice touching each other in romantic but non-sexual ways. It's also fun to learn things together. Practicing your dancing outside of the studio gives couples a chance to engage in a cooperative effort in which they can experience success (or failure) together. Fortunately for our purpose, you can't ballroom dance alone – you need your partner! _If dancing is out of the question, find some activity where you can partner up with your spouse (e.g., bridge clubs, learn a foreign language together so you have someone to practice with, become activists for a cause you both believe in, etc.)._

5. _Surprises_ – (Men) Surprise her with flowers or some other romantic item, maybe a scented candle or a thoughtfully selected greeting card.

6. _Primping_ – (Women) Wear make-up and go the extra mile to look pretty for your guy especially when you are going out on a date. He may not say anything about your new look but he will notice it and appreciate your desire to look nice for him.

7. _Be more agreeable_ – Make a concerted effort to like the things your partner likes. If your partner likes golf, try to like golf. If your partner likes to cook, try to like cooking. You may not succeed in truly liking things you don't already enjoy – the

point is to show your partner you are making an effort to spend time together doing something *he* or *she* likes.

8. *Explore together* – Taking long walks in natural settings usually helps people appreciate the simple things in life including beautiful weather. Partners can enjoy exploring in nature together without having to talk. Comfortably sharing the sounds of silence together is incredibly intimate.

9. *Marvel at the world around you* – Watching the sunset or gazing at the moon are universal pleasures partners can share. These become meaningful moments simply because the view is so grand. These views could never be duplicated – they are special.

10. *Keep your space neat* – Picking up after yourselves so that your partner can be impressed by the way you keep your personal space shows consideration, especially if you've been rather sloppy the past thirty years!

11. *Make special purchases together* – Shopping for things you plan to enjoy together (e.g., a patio swing, a tandem bicycle, season tickets, a dream vacation) triggers happy projections of good times together.

12. *Pursue spiritual growth together* – If you are not inclined to pray together, consider praying together anyway. Any form of spiritual practice is better than nothing as long as one or both of you believes in a Higher Power. If you do not believe in God, discuss philosophy or something that brings personal meaning to your lives.

13. *Be sociable* – Reconnecting with old friends and trying to get together for double dates gives partners opportunities to demonstrate solidarity, thereby reinforcing trust between them.

You can come up with a list of courting ideas on your own. The idea is for partners to do new things together so they can experience each other anew. Even ordinary movie dates can be made special by going to different movie houses or by seeing independent films at your local college-town theater. Try to forget you are married and allow yourselves to get excited about spending time with each other, just as you did when you were first together.

Resolving (presumably) Irreconcilable Differences

"Irreconcilable Differences" is a term divorce lawyers dreamed up. In the past, legally married spouses could not divorce without sufficient grounds. One spouse had to sue the other spouse for divorce based on a legitimate reason for the dissolution of the marriage. Legitimate reasons for divorce included infidelity, imprisonment of one of the spouses, chronic drunkenness, impotence or withholding sex, abandonment, failure to support one's spouse, cruel and abusive treatment, and fraud as it relates to a spouse's true identity or circumstances. Divorcing simply because spouses could not get along was unheard of and an unviable proposition. But nowadays, *irreconcilable differences* is the standard grounds for divorce in the United States.

In families with A.C.E.S., the spouses surely have unresolved differences they have never reconciled which often cause them to exact in an *in-house* divorce. That is, the spouses continue to exist under the same roof but their relationship in no way resembles a healthy marriage.

When marital-partners are too dissimilar, their differing positions on important marital issues can directly impact their ability to live peaceably and happily with one another. Their inability to reconcile their differences disrupts, inhibits or altogether blocks intimacy. A.C.E.S. spouses must be willing to overcome their differences so their marital renovation can continue.

One reason spouses disagree so often is simply because they become competitive with one another over time. Unable to desist in their competitive ways, they may triangulate another person into their relationships so he or she can serve as a peace-maker, lawyer, confessor, or even referee. Spouses may even compete for the triangulated person's love or loyalty. Happily for A.C.E.S. marital-units, by properly examining their differences of opinion on critical matters, spouses can identify ways to meet in the middle and thereby avoid constant arguments, cold wars, violent shouting matches, name calling (which is extremely damaging to marriages), and of course triangulation.

If you've come to the point where you and your spouse are ready to tackle your presumably irreconcilable differences, the level of intimacy you've achieved in the renovation process so far will make resolution of these differences possible and will also provide you with the motivation and willingness necessary to flex for the sake of your marriage.

First, identify whatever differences you think you have. Second, take them one by one and find a way to meet in the middle. It's that simple. When both partners are willing to find resolution on virtually any issue, they amazingly find that they can.

Review the renovation worksheets at the end of each identified topic. Each item should be fully discussed. Thoroughly working through these issues will facilitate the renovation of your marriage.

Completing Renovation Worksheets

Working through the following worksheets will help you sustain your marital renovation.

Each topic represents a potential barrier to intimacy and is identified by a header. Read through each topic together and stop along the way to discuss the questions embedded in the subject at hand. See where you and your spouse can identify with the various assertions and assumptions about your relationship to date. You may find it helpful to journal your thoughts and share them once you've had a chance to consider each item.

Try to maintain objectivity when you come across particularly sensitive subjects that have been a theme in your marital discord. Above all: BE C.O.A.L. *(see Part II, Chapter 1).*

Topic #1 – Finances

It is very important for spouses to speak openly about the financial mistakes they feel they have made. It would be understandably desirable to avoid discussions that would require a spouse to recall his poor investment in a company that manufactured *water-couches*, for example. However, spouses' ability to achieve intimacy is contingent upon their willingness to be entirely open about their faults and failings, including financial failings.

One partner may regret her spending habits that created a tremendous amount of credit-card debt. She may not want to admit her regret to her husband because he had regularly chided her over the years for using credit-cards so freely. She may now feel guilty and ashamed for vigorously defending her spending as justifiable and necessary. In retrospect, she may recognize her spending was more impulsive than necessary but does not want to hear "I told you so" from her husband.

Remember, you are *both* going to admit your financial mistakes to one another so don't waste your time blaming and reproaching each other. Don't say "I told you so" no matter how true it may be. You are trying to come together. You are having a *no-fault* discussion and trying to achieve financial compatibility.

A word of caution when talking about money: make sure to choose an appropriate time to talk. Take it from a marriage counselor, nothing can ignite a fight more quickly than a disagreement about money, particularly if either spouse is already feeling stressed or irritated. Plan to have your financial discussions at a time when you are both calm and relaxed.

I also strongly encourage my A.C.E.S. marital-units to find financial advisors who are objective and neutral. Opinions that come from objective third parties can be incredibly helpful. Financial advisors can facilitate productive discussions that would otherwise turn contentious. Take advantage of their expertise and make use of what they offer by way of financial counsel.

When talking about money, avoid statements that sound accusatory or that place you in a superior position. For example, don't say, "I've always wanted to fund our I.R.A.'s each year. Your credit-card purchases made that impossible." Say something like, "Perhaps we can begin funding our I.R.A.'s again next year. If we work together to cut back on using our credit-cards, I'm sure we can achieve that goal."

Partners who have opted for decades to keep their heads in the sand when it comes to knowing the details of their finances, need to become informed even if their interest in understanding their own financial profile is nil. You may not find finance particularly interesting, but so what? You need to be responsible, informed, and willing to share the burden of managing your finances with your spouse.

Do you know how much money your spouse earned last year? Do you know what his bonus was? What she earned in commissions? What the current balance is in his retirement account? This is all stuff you should know. If you don't know basic information about the money your partner generates, invests, and spends, you and your partner are not financially intimate. There can be no financial secrets in healthy marriages. And opting to remain ignorant of financial matters is as wrong as being financially deceptive. There is no excuse for not taking part in the business of managing your marital finances.

Renovation Worksheet #1 – Finances

1. Do you know the last big purchase your spouse made?
2. Do you know how much it cost?
3. Do you try to hide price tags to avoid being questioned by your spouse as to the necessity of your purchases?
4. Do you hide receipts, snatch incoming credit-card bills from the mailbox or lie about the prices of things you buy?
5. Do you keep separate bank accounts in order to avoid arguments about money?
6. Do you squirrel away money into secret savings accounts so that your spouse can't spend it?
7. Do you hold the purse strings and disallow your spouse from having access to the bank accounts?
8. Are you miserly about money?
9. Do you badger your spouse into reporting the costs of basic household necessities such as food?
10. Do you question every tiny expense and force your spouse to justify modest expenditures?

Depending on how you and your spouse answer these questions, you may need to have some brutally honest discussions about money and how you will proceed to manage it in your newly renovated marriage.

Topic #2 – In-laws

Couples who don't have problems with in-laws probably don't realize how lucky they are!

People can become very sensitive when it comes to members of their original families, and rightly so. No one wants to hear mean statements about her mother – even if the statements are true! It's no fun to hear your father insulted by your spouse, even if your father ruins every party by getting drunk. Partners need to be respectful of each other's feelings for their original family members. It isn't fair to constantly disparage your in-laws no matter how obnoxious, unreasonable, intrusive, or hateful they may be.

If your family of origin is particularly difficult to deal with and you find yourself torn between wanting to please them and wanting to please your spouse, you must err on the side of being loyal to your spouse. Your marital relationship is built on a foundation of a loving commitment to forsake *all* others for the sake of your marriage. Your family of origin falls under the category of *others*. If you find yourself siding with your mother against your husband, something is very wrong. If you find yourself prioritizing the feelings of your father over those of your husband, something is very wrong. If you allow your mother to insult your wife or make your wife feel inadequate or if you allow your mother to dominate your time or interfere with your wife's parenting of your children, something is very, very wrong indeed.

A.C.E.S. spouses must sit down and have a heart-to-heart conversation about the ways their in-laws have impacted their marriage. They must ask each other if they've ever felt threatened by or jealous of one of their in-laws. Have either of you wanted your spouse to defend or support you in disputes with your in-laws only to have your feelings discounted and your requests denied? If the answer is "yes", feeling resentful towards your spouse would be a natural (but destructive) reaction.

When in-laws are allowed to come between two married partners, triangulation ensues. This time it's not your adult-child who is being triangulated, it's your respective in-laws. Remember, triangulation is a generational problem. A.C.E.S. spouses that triangulated their children in their marriage were probably triangulated into the marriages of their own parents. If your in-laws are interfering in your marriage with inappropriate, intrusive behaviors, your spouse has probably not fully de-triangulated from his or her parents. Partners need to support each other when it comes to setting healthy boundaries with their families of origin. Prioritizing each other's feelings will allow partners to feel secure in their relationship. Feeling safe facilitates intimacy and is a marriage renovation necessity.

Renovation Worksheet #2 – In-laws

1. Have your in-laws been a problem in your marriage?
2. Have you felt that your feelings were less important to your spouse than those of his/her parents?
3. How have your in-laws interfered in your marriage?
4. Were you triangulated in your parents' marriage? Are you still triangulated in their marriage? Do you think your spouse was triangulated in his/her parents' marriage? Do you think he/she is still triangulated?
5. If you were the cause of discord between you and your in-laws have you done all you can to repair the damage?
6. How have you tried to set limits and boundaries with your in-laws? Did you feel supported by your spouse when trying to enforce those limits and boundaries?
7. How can we work together to ensure our in-laws don't come between us in the future?

Topic #3 – Friends

The vast majority of my younger clients report having many opposite sex 'friends'. These same clients also report that they are in steady, romantic relationships. I ask how their partners feel about them having so many opposite sex friends and the most common answer to that questions is, "Well he/she has opposite sex friends too so why shouldn't I?" I ask them if they are comfortable with their partners having opposite sex friends. They usually respond, "Well, I'm not going to ask him/her to give up his/her friends. I don't want him/her to think I'm jealous." Good grief!

Perhaps this is a good time to review the characteristics of a friend.

A friend is someone who is trustworthy and caring, someone who is attached to us by feelings of affection and personal regard. A friend is someone we confide in about our internal lives. We reveal ourselves to friends. We rely on friends. We might say something like, "I'm lonely and afraid I'll never find someone to spend my life with" to a friend.

Friendships tend to deepen over time.

Feelings between opposite sex friends can become eroticized over time. The eroticization of a friendship is not necessarily dependent on mutual physical attraction. The *emotional* component of opposite sex friendships is the principle determining factor in whether or not these friendships will become eroticized.

An acquaintance is altogether different from a friend. An acquaintance is someone we talk to about external aspects of our lives. We may say something like, "I can't believe how cold it is outside," to an acquaintance. See the difference?

A friend is someone with whom we share things that are of importance to us. Friends welcome opportunities to do favors for one another. It's normal to ask friends to help us out when we need them. The same is not true of acquaintances.

Acquaintances are people we see on a regular basis because circumstances cause us to be around them. Working in the same place, having children in the same schools, going to the same church…these are all circumstances that would cause people to become acquaintances. Acquaintances become friend-*ly* because they come in frequent contact with each other and both parties are reasonably nice people.

Make no mistake: having opposite sex friends, while in a committed romantic relationship, is foolish and troublesome. In a marriage, opposite sex friendships can lead to infidelity. FYI: Emotional infidelity has the potential to be as damaging to a marriage as physical infidelity.

Married people who are defensive about their rights to have opposite sex friends are protective of their 'friends' because those friends are meeting some of their emotional or spiritual needs. These spouses are outsourcing their needs to people outside of their marriages and A.C.E.S. marital-units need to stop maintaining opposite sex friendships if they are going to establish intimacy in their relationships.

As a marriage therapist, it saddens me when I hear that spouses are more fearful about *sounding* jealous than they are about protecting the integrity of their marriages. False pride is at work here and partners need to stop relinquishing *legitimate* territorial rights over their spouses. Your husband or wife should be able to satisfy your opposite sex internal needs. You can surely get some of your spiritual and emotional needs met through same sex friendships which would be healthy and appropriate.

Ask one another if you've ever been reluctant to express your feelings about your spouse's opposite sex friendships because of false pride. Openly discuss your feelings about hurts and frustrations over your partner's turning to another man/woman for support, comfort, or guidance. Discuss whether you are willing to make the commitment not to socialize with opposite sex friends unless your spouse is involved. Agree to delete or "de-friend" opposite sex friends from your social networking pages. Take a history of occurrences of opposite sex friendships in your relationship and speak freely about how those friendships compromised your marriage. Finally, draw a distinction between the friends and acquaintances in your lives and make a commitment to distance yourselves from all opposite sex friends going forward. Unless an opposite sex friend is one half of a couple you and your spouse socialize with together, let go of the relationship. Do not speak on the phone, get together for coffee or a meal, meet up for a walk, exchange text messages or emails. These are all intimate activities.

The integrity of your marriage is contingent upon the establishment of intimacy with your spouse. If you outsource your spiritual or emotional needs to opposite sex friends, you will triangulate him or her into your marriage and doing so could be catastrophic to your marriage.

One more thing about friends: you may need to seriously consider your spouse's feelings about your same sex friends. If your spouse has a legitimate problem with one of your same sex friends, you need to be open to discussing whether or not the friendship should be continued. For example, if my husband's buddy liked to go to get drunk and go to strip clubs with my husband in tow, I would demand that my husband end the friendship on the grounds that his friend's behavior is destructive and offensive to me both personally and interpersonally. If I had a girlfriend who engaged in routine romantic affairs with married men and my husband objected to our friendship on the grounds that her behavior was immoral and destructive to families, I would have to respect his feelings on the matter.

On the other hand, if I didn't like one of my husband's buddies because he chewed tobacco and was always spitting, or if my husband didn't like one of my friends because she had an obnoxious laugh, we would have to work out an agreement about how to maintain our friendships without causing each other to be uncomfortable. It would not be necessary for either of us to terminate our friendships for superficial reasons.

In sum, we want to always be respectful and considerate of our spouses and their feelings regardless of the issue. In terms of questionable friends who may or may not be coming between you and your partner, a lot of listening and a bit of sensitivity will be very helpful when you tackle this portion of the renovation process.

Renovation Worksheet #3 – Friends

1. Have friends come between you and your spouse?
2. Have you felt less important to your spouse than his or her friend(s)?
3. Have you been guilty of outsourcing your emotional needs to an opposite sex friend?
4. Do you maintain opposite sex friendships on social networking sites on the Internet? At work? In other social settings?
5. Have you been straightforward with your feelings about your spouse's opposite sex friendships?
6. Are you unjustifiably jealous of casual acquaintances?
7. Have you refused to meet your spouse's emotional needs thereby provoking him or her to seek emotional support from an opposite sex friend?
8. Do you have issues with some of your spouse's same sex friends? Why do you object to your spouse's friendships with these particular people?
9. Are you willing to forsake destructive friendships for the sake of your marriage? If not, why not?
10. Can you be more tolerant of your spouse's same sex friends that are harmless to your relationship, even if you personally don't like those particular friends?
11. Do you understand what it means to *forsake all others* for the sake of the marriage? Individually explain your understanding of "forsaking all others."
12. Will you forsake all others for the sake of your marriage?

Topic #4 – Careers

It's important to address how to fix career related marital problems for your marriage renovation to be successful. Chances are that you and your spouse addressed the topic of careers before you got married but you probably did not anticipate the sorts of challenges those careers would bring to your marriage. For example, marrying a doctor may certainly have its advantages. But the sacrifices involved in being the spouse of a doctor can be enormous. In fact, many people who marry doctors find that the sacrifices are too great and their marriages end in divorce. Or perhaps you married a *'starving artist'*, believing that his talent would one day be discovered and that the two of you would eventually live carefree lives. You never imagined that you'd end up resenting your artistic spouse for not working a 'regular' job in order to provide your family with stability and security.

Even couples that address career issues thoroughly prior to marriage can get blindsided by unforeseen career related circumstances. While you cannot be faulted for neglecting to plan for every conceivable career contingency prior to marriage, any career related problem that surfaced at some point during the marriage must now be resolved. The marital renovation requires A.C.E.S. marital-units to work through all the potential barriers to intimacy, including career related problems.

Despite the obvious problems career issues may have caused (are causing) in your marriage, you and your spouse may feel that you are limited in what you can do about them now. It may have taken decades to achieve certain measures of professional success and it could be very difficult to make significant career adjustments at this stage of your lives.

Over the years, you may have made many personal sacrifices in order to climb the ranks in your field. You may have attained a lifestyle that is pleasing to you and your family. Perhaps you fear making changes that might require you to give up what you worked so hard to realize (e.g., prestige, possessions, power, security). But at this point, when having a happy marriage hangs in the balance, you may have to consider making at least some modest career related changes.

One thing that can be done immediately is for the two of you to come together on the motivating factors behind maintaining the status quo as it relates to career related matters. If you both consciously decide, for example, to sacrifice time together now in order to retire early, so be it. Your goal is to find the *same* motivation so that you can support each other in your joint *sacrifice* of not spending time together in the present day.

There are always things that can be done to make a bad situation a bit better. Too much time apart is generally not good for marriages, but if there is no practical way to avoid being apart, look for other ways to connect during those times. You may be able to generate some long-distance intimacy in the fashion of yesteryear (e.g., handwritten letters, sending small gifts in the mail, etc.). How romantic!

If your answers to the questions below lead you to believe that one or both of your careers have become barriers in establishing an intimate marriage, put your heads together and find ways to circumvent the barriers.

Renovation Sheet #4 – Careers

1. To begin with, reflect on your financial profile as it relates to your careers. Without discussing anything, get an idea in your own minds where you are financially in terms of stability, etc.
2. Does your career bring meaning to your life? How so?
3. Do you resent your spouse's career? How so?
4. Are you jealous of your spouse's career success?
5. Are you frustrated by your spouse's financial power in your relationship simply because he or she makes more money than you do?
6. Do you feel inferior because your spouse earns more than you do or has a more prestigious career?
7. Are you depressed because you are unhappy in your career? Has this dissatisfaction interfered in your marital relationship?
8. Are you working to make ends meet, build financial security, or are you establishing an empire?
9. Are you motivated to work more because you trying to pay off debt? If so, what are the debts? Do you work too much because you are worried about money?
10. Are you saving for a luxury item like a brand new sports car? Is your spouse aware that you want to buy such an item? Does he or she approve of your desire to splurge on an expensive luxury item exclusively for your own enjoyment?
11. Are you or is your spouse a "work-a-holic"? Has your spouse begged you to not work so much? Have you pleaded with your spouse to cut back on overtime in order to spend more time with you?
12. What are the specific career components that have interfered in your relationship? For example, does your position place you in danger? Are you frequently 'on call'? Is it impossible

to get away from your business because no one else can do your job?

13. Is your work the only part of your life that makes you feel successful?

14. Is your self-worth wrapped up in how well you perform at work?

15. Have you *freely* chosen to work rather than spend time with your spouse? Why?

16. Are travelling requirements causing you to spend too much time apart? Do you engage in immoral behavior when you are away from your spouse on long trips? Has that deception interfered in your ability to be intimate with your spouse? Are you consumed with guilt over your behavior? *(If you answered "yes" to the last three questions, it would be wise not to discuss them with your spouse. It isn't fair to burden your spouse with details that would hurt him or her. Rather, you should talk these things over with another person in order to process your regret, etc.)*

17. Is working long hours a standard requirement of your position?

18. Is your work so stressful that it dominates your thoughts and prevents you from being emotionally present in your marriage?

19. Is your free time frequently interrupted by your job?

20. Do you own your own company and need to spend most of your waking hours there to keep the operation on its feet?

21. Does your career give you more satisfaction than your marriage? If yes, how so?

22. Are you willing to do what it takes to modify your career related issues that have negatively affected your marriage?

Topic #5 – Spirituality

The most intimate part of the marital renovation process involves spirituality. Whether you and your spouse connect spiritually through mutual faith in a Higher Power or through meaningful pursuits that strengthen your marital bond, you will realize great marital satisfaction when your relationship involves a spiritual component.

Let's face it – A.C.E.S. all but decimates marital satisfaction. Finding meaningful ways for spouses to connect is the goal in overcoming their spiritual barrier to intimacy. Spouses can begin their search for mutual meaningful purpose by answering the following questions and discussing their answers together.

Renovation Worksheet #5 – Spirituality

God Questions

1. Do you believe in God? (*If the answer to this question is "no",
   skip all the God-related questions*).
2. Do you and your spouse believe in the same God?
3. Do you feel uncomfortable talking about God?
4. Do you feel resentful towards God or your religion?
5. Do you feel disdain for people who believe in God?
6. Did you once believe in God? Did you lose faith after
   a devastating loss or because you found your religion too
   stringent?
7. Do you rely on God? How so?
8. Do you pray? When? How?
9. Would you feel comfortable praying with your spouse?
10. Has your relationship with God changed over the years? How
    so?
11. How do you feel about attending religious/spiritual services
    (e.g., Church, Temple, meditative retreat houses, etc?)
12. (*If you attend religious/spiritual services*) Do you feel connected
    to one another when you go to church, temple, spiritual centers,
    or do you feel that you are "going through the motions"?
13. Do you think you can come to know God as a couple? Is this
    something you want to do? Why or why not?

Meaningful Pursuits

1. What do you do that makes you feel good about who you are?
2. What do you do that makes you feel peaceful?
3. Do you have an unfulfilled desire to offer yourself in service to a cause you believe in?
4. Do you have a particular interest in any charitable organizations? Would you like to volunteer time working for those organizations?
5. Who do you admire? Why?
6. Do you feel you have something to offer to the world that you have been keeping to yourself?

Meaningful Purpose

1. Are you lonely? Do you feel a lack of meaningful purpose in your life? In your marriage?
2. What do you think you are meant to do with your life? Are you doing that? If not, why not?
3. As spouses, do you think you have mutual purpose now that you've raised your children?
4. Do you feel like you are growing on a personal level? How so or why not?
5. Do you feel stagnant or unfulfilled?
6. Are you burdened with numerous life regrets? Do you doubt that your life has had purpose thus far?

Secret Fears

Sharing one's deepest fears with another human being can create a spiritual bond between those two people that, prior to doing so, never even existed. Most people are hesitant to talk about their deepest fears because doing so will inevitably place them in very vulnerable interpersonal positions with the people they decide to trust. Revealing our fears to another is an indication of true trust in the other person's ability to react with tenderness and non-judgment of who we truly are. Sharing of self with others is an indisputable risk as people are unpredictable creatures. We cannot be sure how others will react to us once we've revealed ourselves. We can never be absolutely certain that we will not be judged, belittled, or dismissed. We may not achieve the validation, warmth and comfort we are seeking and that can be painfully disappointing depending on whom we decide to trust with our feelings. But when we are willing to expose our humanity to our *spouses* by trusting them with our innermost thoughts, we will surely deepen our spiritual connection and more fully establish intimacy in our marriages.

The following are questions related to your innermost fears. Be gentle as you probe one another about your personal fears. Remember, these are thoughts you've never fully shared with each other. It isn't likely that you are going to divulge the contents of your very souls in one fell swoop. Be patient and loving as you work through this section of questions.

1. What are your fears?
2. What causes you to despair and feel hopeless?
3. Are you afraid of something your spouse doesn't know about? Are you willing to share it with your spouse?
4. Do you feel like your spouse could never understand your fears? Are you afraid your spouse will discount your fears or minimize them?
5. Do you sometimes feel empty inside? Do you keep those thoughts to yourself because you think your spouse won't care or won't understand?
6. Have you tried to share your fears with your spouse in the past only to go away disappointed by your spouse's reaction?

It will probably take you weeks or months to answer all the questions that pertain to spirituality. These discussions should only happen in relaxed settings when time constraints are not an issue. There is no rush to get through these questions! Just keep having these *types* of discussions.

In terms of your own spirituality, you may learn as much about yourself as you will about your spouse. If you continue addressing spiritual matters, there is no way to avoid drawing closer as partners. Over time, your spiritual barrier to intimacy will be eliminated.

Topic #6 – Health Matters

Issues related to your health or the health of your spouse can absolutely interfere with your ability to establish and maintain intimacy in your marriage. Health issues may include weight problems, serious medical conditions, untreated mental health problems such as depression or anxiety, or chemical or behavioral addictions such as alcoholism or gambling *(see Part I, Chapter 3 for more information about the role of addiction as it pertains to the development of A.C.E.S.).*

Fear of being abandoned by one's partner is certainly a barrier to intimacy. We can experience physical, emotional, spiritual, or sexual abandonment via death, chronic sickness, or addiction. When a partner is able to regularly observe his or her spouse neglecting his or her health, a subconscious fear of abandonment can be triggered. When one's partner is reckless with his or her health, feelings of resentment and hostility towards him or her are likely to develop. For example, if a husband recklessly neglects his health, his wife might conclude, *"He obviously doesn't love me or he wouldn't keep eating like that. He has high cholesterol and he's sitting there eating a can of peanuts."*

If you are neglecting your health, carefully consider how your behavior is impacting your spouse's ability to trust your loving commitment to her/him. Let your partner share her/his feelings about how you care for yourself and be willing to take steps to become more conscientious about your health. When the changes you make in the department of self-care become evident to your spouse, you will likely notice increases in loving support, devotion and intimacy in your marriage.

Renovation Worksheet #6 – Health Matters

1. Do you have a health condition that is affecting your marriage?
2. Is your health interrupting precious aspects of married life, such as the ability and desire to engage in sexual activity?
3. Has your health kept you from participating in activities that you and your spouse would otherwise enjoy together?
4. Has your spouse expressed concern about your health? Have you taken his/her feelings to heart?
5. Have you tried, unsuccessfully, to conquer your health issue? What have you tried and why do you think it did not work?
6. What are you willing to do now to address and remedy your health issue?
7. If your spouse has health issues that are interfering in your marriage, how have you addressed your concerns with him/her?
8. Have you used guilt and shame to manipulate your spouse into fixing his/her health issues?
9. Have you tried bribing your spouse in order to get him/her to fix his/her health issues? What kinds of things have you promised him/her? Why do you think this tactic did not motivate your spouse to take positive actions regarding his/her health?
10. Do you both have health issues that interfere with your marriage? If so, do you use the fact that your partner hasn't addressed his/her health issues to justify the fact that you have neglected your own health?

11. Are you willing to support your spouse in addressing his/her health issues without trying to control or monitor him/her?
12. Will you practice loving compassion and tolerance when your spouse fails to progress at a pace you'd like?
13. Will you do your best to not become defensive when your spouse expresses loving concern about your health?

Topic #7 – Household Business

A.C.E.S. spouses often present with frustration over feelings that they are doing more than their fair share of the household duties. They become angry, resentful, and ultimately hostile towards their partners when they feel things are not equitable regarding household business. Household business refers to housework, scheduling appointments, cooking, shopping, running errands, managing finances and paying bills, coordinating children's schedules, and the like. I explain to partners that their frustrations are stemming from the fear of being taken for granted and the belief that their efforts are not appreciated. It's basically an issue of pride.

A lot of times A.C.E.S. spouses have irrational and unreasonable expectations for each other that cause them to become mutually resentful. Practically speaking, it may make sense for a particular partner to take care of certain household responsibilities merely because of logistics. For example, if a husband doesn't get home until 7 PM because he has a two-hour commute from work, he probably would not be able to get dinner on the table by 6 PM for the family. Therefore, resenting him for never cooking dinner doesn't make much sense. Likewise, if a wife works fulltime and also does the bulk of the childcare, it is highly unrealistic to expect her to also do all of the housework. Resenting her because the home is messy is unfair. One can only do so much and partners need to be supportive and understanding of one another's limitations. They also need to work together to solve common problems which pertain to ongoing responsibilities such as household business.

When it comes to household business, the idea is to be sure to give your spouse the validation and appreciation he or she deserves for doing the things that keep the household afloat. Try to notice when the house has been freshly cleaned or when the trash makes its way to the curb. Don't hold back on offering gratitude simply because you think your spouse is merely doing what he or she is *supposed* to do anyway. That's called *'taking someone for granted'*.

Factually speaking, people can't really be forced to do things they don't want to do. They may suffer consequences (including death or bodily harm) for failing to do certain things but it is still their choice whether or not to do it. Believe me, there is no *'crazy'* like the *'crazy'* that comes from trying to control others! Despite your greatest efforts, you will find that it cannot be done. Regrettably, people frustrate themselves needlessly when they make it their business to control other human beings. Fortunately, if you and your spouse can maintain a spirit of cooperation with the common goal of achieving an orderly household, you will be able to divvy up the chores in an equitable fashion without succumbing to coercion.

Recognize that the goal is not to measure your partner's contribution or to compare his contribution to yours. It's about cooperating with the intention of achieving a common goal. Partners run into trouble on this issue when their goals, priorities, and preferences are not aligned. For example, if one spouse is not bothered by clutter and the other is a 'neat-freak', they have a misaligned preference. This is where the art of compromise comes becomes relevant.

In my own marriage, I'm the one who prefers the house to be tidy. My husband doesn't seem to mind clutter on the tables and counter tops but it drives me crazy to see mail piled up on the kitchen table and dirty dishes on the counters. So the compromise we developed is that he will (try to) keep the kitchen table cleared off and at least clear the dishes off the counters and put them in the sink or dishwasher. In return, I agreed to stop nagging him about his messy desktop. It's his desk. I hate the way it looks but it's out of sight from most of the house. If we're going to have a true compromise, I can't expect my husband to keep *all* surfaces free of clutter because he couldn't care less about clutter. It is an effort for him to keep certain surfaces clutter-free, and when he does, he does it to please me. In the same way, he can't expect me to simply accept that there is clutter all over the place. He knows I can't stand it when the main parts of the house look messy. My compromise is that I don't harass him about how he keeps his personal space. Simply put, my husband has to adjust to my need for a fair amount of tidiness and I have to adjust to his desire to maintain a disorderly mess of a desk (*just kidding; I couldn't resist a bit of sarcasm here!!*).

Now I need to tell you that this compromise between my husband and myself has not *always* been fool proof (far from it). However, it makes us feel better to have an agreement in place. When you have an agreement that isn't being honored, it would be fine to say "Is the agreement we made about _____ still in place? Can I count on you to recommit to doing _____? Thank you. It's important to me and I appreciate your doing that to make me happy."

In order to maintain a peaceful household and to stave off the re-accumulation of resentments, I always encourage partners to ask for help when they need it. If you are truly overwhelmed by a disproportionate volume of things to do around the house, say so. Don't be a martyr and suffer in silence. And don't be a nag. Just let your spouse know you are feeling overwhelmed. It may turn out that some things must go undone for the time being. Try to identify a list of 'must-dos' and be sure to tackle those things first. In fact, go ahead and enlist your spouse to help you prioritize your tasks. Appeal to your spouse's ego by soliciting his or her advice, support, and assistance. Let him or her help solve the problem.

Definitely be *specific* if you need help with a particular task. Saying things like "Can you help pick up the house?" won't work. Say something like "There's a bunch of folded laundry on the couch. Will you please put the towels in the linen closet and the clothes away in our dresser drawers?" You'll almost always get a better result if you're specific about your requests.

One last thing: don't let your spouse's negative reaction to your requests prevent you from asking for or *accepting* his or her help. Many of my clients report that when their spouses grumble about one of their requests, they (my clients) say things like "Forget it…I'll do it myself." That is awfully silly. Let your spouse grumble! That isn't a crime. As long as your spouse is willing to do whatever it is you've asked him or her to do, your part is done. Why should you be the martyr who does all the work? If your spouse isn't overjoyed to do the dishes, that's fine. The point is that you need your spouse to do the dishes. The darn dishes need to be washed and, for *whatever* reason, you aren't able to wash them. As long as the dishes get done, your spouse can have any attitude he or she likes about helping you. Unless your spouse is throwing things, slamming doors and drawers, yelling like a lunatic, or being otherwise obnoxious, just accept his or her lousy attitude and move on. All you have to do is smile, say "thank you", and *be nice*. Don't offer a sarcastic *'thank you'* and don't *over* thank your spouse. Just say "thank you" in a nice but unemotional tone.

If your spouse's attitude about sharing household business is extremely negative, or if your spouse only helps out grudgingly, you should discuss it. But be sure to only discuss the attitude. This would not be the time to argue about specific chores, etc. Your conversation should start like this: "I'm starting to feel very uncomfortable by the way you react when I ask you to help with household business. Please help me to understand your reactions to reasonable requests for help."

When you have some time to talk about household business, you may begin by asking each other the questions on the next renovation worksheet.

Renovation Worksheet #7 – Household Business

1. Do you think the way you and your spouse distribute your household responsibilities is fair?
2. Do you feel that you are taken for granted or unappreciated when it comes to doing household chores?
3. Do you want your spouse to do more? What specifically can your spouse do to make household business more equitable?
4. Do you feel a lot of pressure to make things perfect? Would you be willing to let some things slide in favor of keeping a peaceful household?
5. What are the things you thoroughly resent having to do? Can you and your spouse trade off on doing the really loathsome chores?
6. Would you and your spouse be willing to farm out some of your household business to a gardener, housekeeper, pool cleaner, business manager, etc.? If not, why not? If the added expense prevents you from outsourcing household business, can you and your spouse cut back in other areas to afford something that will help keep peace in the household?
7. Will you make more of an effort to offer praise and appreciation for the things your spouse does?
8. Would you be willing to identify specific times that you and your spouse take care of household business together? Can you make commitments to do those things at those times?
9. Can you and your spouse agree on a list of things that need to be done on a weekly basis, monthly basis, quarterly basis, and yearly basis and schedule particular days to get those things done?

You will be surprised by the reduction in tension between the two of you when you both start feeling more appreciation and cooperation. And, hopefully, the house will run smoother and be a more peaceful place to live.

Topic #8 – Childcare (if still an issue)

While your adult-child may be on his way to achieving personal responsibility, you may still have younger children at home who need to be looked after. As you have learned, one parent having too much involvement with any given child may lead to triangulation of that child. In an A.C.E.S. family, if one parent is predominantly involved in the lives of the younger children, it would be wise for the other parent to increase his involvement now and for the other parent to step back a bit *now.*

You are equally responsible for the development of your children. When A.C.E.S. marital-units feel that they are co-parenting as a team it enhances marital intimacy. The spouses are more supportive of each other and ultimately feel closer. Perhaps most importantly, they present a united front to their children who fare better when they see their parents as a stable unit.

Discuss your answers to the questions on the following renovation worksheet with your spouse when you both have time to thoughtfully consider your feelings.

Renovation Worksheet #8 – Childcare

1. Would you be willing to let your spouse occasionally share in the special things you normally do alone with your child?
2. When your child has a problem, would you be willing to redirect her to your spouse in order to foster balance in your child's relationships with you and your spouse?
3. Would you be willing to take over some of the childcare responsibilities such as taking them to the doctor or to afterschool activities when you can? Will you be more helpful when it comes to homework and school projects? Would you be willing to join your spouse in enforcing household rules (i.e., not let things slide when your spouse is not around)?
4. Will you consult with your spouse before making significant decisions that pertain to your children?
5. Will you work with your spouse to find a disciplinary style you can both agree upon?
6. Will you abstain from talking about the problems you have with your spouse with your children?
7. Will you avoid making disparaging remarks about your spouse to your children?
8. Do you feel jealous of the time your spouse spends alone with your children?
9. Do you regret not being around much when your children were younger?
10. What would you do differently with your children if you had the chance?
11. Do you feel it is too late to change course with your younger children?

12. When it comes to correcting your children, will you try to avoid disagreeing with your spouse in front of them?

13. Can you and your spouse present yourselves to your children as a unit?

14. Will you work with your spouse to de-triangulate your children from your marriage?

Clearly, the last of these questions is the most important if you are to avoid a repeat occurrence of A.C.E.S. The two of you will do yourselves, and your *future* adult-children, a world of good if you make your expectations clear to your children and you enforce consequences for failure to adhere to your rules. When the two of you present yourselves as a stable unit to your children (young or adult) they will be more likely to differentiate themselves from you, a critical aspect of becoming independent adults. Your consistency in this area will positively impact their behaviors and attitudes for the rest of their lives.

Topic #9 – Marital Goals

Marriages are much like businesses in that marriages and businesses are cooperative organizations with various functional requirements. Both marriages and businesses are legally established entities. Both entities are required to have state licenses in order to be recognized as valid. Without a doubt, there are legitimate similarities between marriages and businesses.

But, and appropriately so, businesses and marriages don't *function* exactly the same way. Businesses, for the most part, thrive in the realm of rationality and practicality. Marriages do better when sensitivity, spirituality, and sensuality (among other things) are added to the mix. However, many marriages would benefit from adopting at least one best practice of business and that is to *identify clear and measurable goals.*

The first goal of any success-bound business is to identify its mission. What is the business going to do? Will it sell a product or service? Will it directly serve the public or will its interactions be done business-to-business? Is the company going to be a global operation or a local business on Main Street? Will the business be a non-profit organization driven by an altruistic cause? How is the business going to be managed? How will the business be different from its competitors?

The answers to questions like these make up typical content of mission statements for businesses. Serious businesses that are determined to succeed usually go to the trouble of *writing* their mission statements down. They print them in training manuals, put them on company plaques, or take excerpts from their mission statements and turn those excerpts into company slogans. The reason businesses do this is because smart business owners want to be reminded of *what they are trying to accomplish,* lest they get distracted from their primary purpose. Business owners are the officers of their companies. They are the ones most focused on realizing the mission statements of their businesses.

You and your spouse are the owners of your marriage. You would be wise to emulate good business practice and write a mission statement for your marriage. See if answering the questions on the next renovation worksheet can help you and your spouse develop a mission statement of your own.

Renovation Worksheet #9 – Marital Goals

1. Are you 100% committed to creating a marriage that is mutually rewarding and satisfying?
2. Can you define the foundation of your marriage? What is it?
3. What do you value and does your marriage reflect those values?
4. How are you and your spouse, as a unit, contributing to the wellness of your society as a whole?
5. Do you and your spouse pursue meaningful purpose as a married couple? How so?
6. Do you and your spouse interact in such a way as to reflect a healthy and loving marriage around others? Is your marriage an example of a healthy relationship?
7. Do you and your spouse (as a unit) make yourselves available to others in need?
8. Are you and your spouse committed to personal growth in the spirit of becoming better partners to one another? How do you demonstrate your commitment to growing as a couple?
9. How do you and your spouse address and correct your failures as a couple?
10. Do you and your spouse live out your marriage vows? In other words, do you actively honor, cherish, and love one another?

Chapter Summary

The point of marital renovation is to make your marriage better in every way possible! Follow the guidelines in this chapter and watch what happens: ***"...you will be amazed before you are halfway through."*** This quote was taken from page 83 of <u>*Alcoholics Anonymous*</u> otherwise known as *'The Big Book'*.

Chapter 4 – Phase 4: Reduce the Potential for an A.C.E.S. Relapse

Even after a seemingly stellar recovery from A.C.E.S., it is not only *possible* for a relapse to occur, it is likely. That is a reality that A.C.E.S. families must be aware of if they plan to beat the odds of experiencing relapses (or re-occurrences of A.C.E.S. with other adult-children). The best way for you and your family to avoid a relapse is to *strictly* follow the A.C.E.S. program of recovery outlined in this book. Secondly, you and your fellow family members must commit to doing everything possible to continue on your *personal* paths to recovery. You must continue to monitor your personal behaviors, attitudes, and feelings and consciously reject negative inclinations to return to destructive patterns.

Your first step in avoiding an A.C.E.S. relapse is for you and your family to understand and recognize the four most common relapse triggers.

> ## Relapse Trigger #1
> Continuous Emotional Tension in the Marriage

In the early going, the most common relapse trigger for marital-units is an ongoing struggle to cope with emotional tension in their marriages. For some A.C.E.S. marital-units, building sufficient levels of marital intimacy (necessary to prevent the re-triangulation of their adult-children) may take considerably longer than the amount of time it took to launch their adult-children into the world.

Even when couples have been successful in increasing levels of marital intimacy during the preparation for launch and marital renovation processes, they may still fall into the trap of wanting to triangulate others if only by force of habit. After all, it is not easy to change. It is perfectly natural to slip into old behavioral patterns once in a while. Anyone who has ever tried to lose weight knows how hard it is to *permanently* change certain behaviors!

Couples who have triangulated others in the past will always need to monitor their automatic inclinations to triangulate again. The tendency to triangulate does not go away permanently simply because couples abstain from triangulating behaviors for a period of time. It's important to understand that couples don't consciously triangulate others into their relationships. Triangulation is a *sub*conscious *reaction* to interpersonal stress. That is to say that the behaviors associated with triangulation happen automatically in response to relationship tension. Therefore, when stressors occur in marital relationships, partners may instinctually look to ease the tension by what has worked for them in the past: triangulation.

Marital-units should periodically take the following '*triangulation inventory*' in order to measure their current levels of triangulatory attitudes and behaviors. Depending on the results of their triangulation inventories, partners can either maintain the status quo or change course. If they find they have slipped into old dysfunctional behavioral patterns, they can take steps to reconnect in healthy ways.

Triangulation Inventory – (Answer True or False)

1. Lately, I have preferred to speak to someone other than my spouse about things that are directly related to him or her.
2. I have been communicating with my spouse through another person.
3. Lately, I have been feeling that it is easier to keep my thoughts to myself than to share them with my spouse.

4. I feel more comfortable admitting my thoughts to someone other than my spouse.

5. Lately, when my spouse and I have had opportunities to spend time alone together, I have wanted to include my adult-child or other individuals.

6. My spouse has been bugging me lately.

7. My adult-child has been using me to communicate with my spouse and I haven't put a stop to it.

8. Lately, I feel more comfortable around my spouse when others are present.

More than one or two 'True' responses to the above statements may indicate an increase in your susceptibility to triangulation. In order to keep relapse trigger #1 at bay, revisit ways to rekindle intimacy in your marriage and distance yourself from '*triangulatable-others*'.

Relapse Trigger #2
Homesickness

Homesickness may be a relapse trigger for many adult-children. Symptoms of homesickness include phoning parents frequently at home, work, or on their cell phones, visiting often, sleeping over when they could just as easily go home, and tearfulness over missing their parents and younger siblings. The most obvious symptom of homesickness is a direct request to move home on the part of the homesick person (i.e., the adult-child).

Homesickness may seem to come on quite suddenly with some adult-children. Initially, adult-children may not feel the least bit homesick because the transition into independent living is very distracting and can temporarily overshadow the melancholy feelings so typical of homesickness.

As most adults can remember, the happy distraction of one's new found independence can feel exhilarating! In many cases, living independently can produce positive new behaviors and better attitudes about day-to-day living. It is often the case that newly independent adult-children, who behaved like slobs when living at their parents' homes, become neat freaks when tending to their own spaces. The natural pride they feel when they take ownership of their new lives may reveal undiscovered traits such as tidiness, frugality, good time management, and even respect for the property of others! In fact, once adult-children achieve financial independence, they may come to truly appreciate the luxuries their parents provided for them all the years they lived at home.

But once the novelty of life on their own wanes, the reality of monthly bills, cooking, cleaning, shopping, and developing a new social support system to replace the built-in support system they enjoyed at home with their parents, sets in and overwhelms many adult-children. Those overwhelming feelings are manifested in what appears to be homesickness.

A.C.E.S. parents and adult-children alike must anticipate the possibility that, at some point, homesickness might trigger the desire to return to the nest. Adult-children should not allow themselves to be blindsided by the faulty notion that the homesickness will not pass. Likewise, A.C.E.S. parents should not entertain feelings of excessive sympathy. Everyone will be okay. It's important to "ride out" the homesickness and stay the course. In time, it will not even be an issue.

<u>Relapse Trigger #3</u>
Not Having Contingency Plans

There are two well-known expressions that come to mind when I reflect upon relapse trigger #3. The first of these expressions is "If you fail to plan, you plan to fail." The other is "Anything that can go wrong, will go wrong." That second one certainly sounds a bit defeatist, but it often times (too often) seems to be a true statement. I have called reference to these two well-known expressions for a reason: well-known expressions become well-known because they are often true.

After the adult-child in an A.C.E.S. family has been launched, everyone is usually filled with high hopes. Each member of the family worked hard to overcome the family dilemma of A.C.E.S. and all are motivated to make the new regime stick. But let's face it, things happen. Obviously, we cannot plan for every contingency that could interfere with permanent A.C.E.S. recovery. However, we can make plans as to how we would deal with unexpected predicaments.

Below is a list of such predicaments and you may want to keep an eye out for any and all of them. It would be wise to have contingency plans in place if any of these situations present themselves as they could prompt a return to the nest for a *child-like* adult-child.

1. A roommate who is paying rent suddenly moves out leaving the A.C.E.S. adult-child in a financial pickle.
2. The adult-child suddenly loses his or her job.
3. An A.C.E.S. parent becomes ill, compelling the adult-child to help the other parent with healthcare responsibilities.
4. The adult-child goes through an emotionally difficult time (e.g., ending a long-term relationship with a boyfriend or girlfriend would be considered an emotionally difficult time) and has become very lonely.
5. The adult-child is very unhappy in his or her living situation causing the A.C.E.S. parents to become overly sympathetic which in turn prompts their impulse to rescue their son or daughter with an invitation to move home.

I'm not going to take the time to create contingency plans for the situations above. You can (*and should*) do that on your own. I'm speaking to the adult-child when I say, "*Having a back-up plan, in case something goes wrong, is part of being a responsible adult.*"

It should not be difficult to create a simple contingency plan for each potential predicament. Many will only be a sentence or two long. These plans should be written in the plainest of terms. I suggest that adult-children write down their plans in the following format: "If _____ happens, my plan is to _____." Some adult-children may want to include a self-affirming statement such as, "I will not move home even if _____ happens because I will be able to handle it on my own."

Relapse Trigger #4
Providing Adult-children with Financial Bail-outs

Most everyone needs help from time to time. Financial emergencies do arise and can cause people to panic. On the other hand, financial emergencies can also cause people to discover how resourceful they can actually be.

Relapse trigger #4 is entirely avoidable as long as A.C.E.S. adult-children understand that they *will be required* to solve their financial emergencies without the financial aid of their parents. An adult-child may need to borrow money, but it should not be borrowed from Mom and Dad. While asking Mom and Dad for a loan may be the easiest way to avoid financial catastrophe, it would not be the smartest way given its potential to trigger an A.C.E.S. relapse.

The last thing A.C.E.S. families want to do is to reestablish the dysfunctional precedent of rescuing able-bodied adult-children. To do so would suggest that A.C.E.S. marital-units are still resources that could be tapped at will.   Non-emergencies may be perceived as *actual* emergencies by your adult-child. He may go to you for 'emergency' funds as you have helped him financially throughout his adult life. He is likely to do this before he explores other ways to get the money he needs on his own (e.g., getting a second or third job, etc.).

An A.C.E.S. adult-child who is bound for relapse would be happy to accept money from his parents rather than earn it himself. Relapse-bound A.C.E.S. parents may be torn about whether to A) lend their adult-child money, B) allow him to move home, or C) let him find his own financial solution. A relapse would officially take place if A.C.E.S. parents chose items A or B.

As previously stated, finding one's own solutions for one's own problems is a necessary part of maturing into a responsible adult. It is absolutely critical that adult-children take responsibility for themselves financially. As discussed in Chapter 2 of Part II in this book, it is okay to be helpful when your adult-child seeks you out for help, but it is very important that you utilize the method of Socratic Questioning *(see Step 7 in Chapter 1 of Part II)* to help her identify her own solutions to her problems. Let me give you an example:

Adult-daughter: "Mom, I need to borrow a thousand dollars for old parking tickets on my car. If I don't pay the fine they are going to impound my car."

Mom: "Wow, that's a lot of money! What's your plan?"

Adult-daughter: "Well, can you lend me the money?"

Mom: "Is that your plan?"

Adult-daughter: "Mom, I don't have anyone else to ask. Please."

Mom: "You sound really worried. What are your other options if you aren't able to borrow the money?"

Adult-daughter: "Mom, I don't have any other options. That's why I'm coming to you."

Mom: "I'm sure there are other options. I can think of a few. Why don't we give this some thought?"

Adult-daughter: "Mom, are you going to lend me the money or not?"

Mom: "I'm willing to be helpful. Do you think if I lend you money it will be helpful?"

Adult-daughter: "Yes, Mom! Stop messing with me. I need the money!"

Mom: "I know you do! I believe you, honey. Do you want my help making a plan?"

Adult-daughter: "No, just forget it. I'll figure this out on my own."

EXACTLY!!!

Now in a case where you feel that a financial arrangement could be made that would include your adult-child putting up collateral and paying back a loan with interest, you may choose to do so. But that would be risky. Chances are your adult-child doesn't have any collateral that would be worth anything to you if he were to default on a loan. And I seriously doubt that any A.C.E.S. parent would be up to taking her adult-child to court over a money dispute! Why not avoid the whole thing by allowing your adult-child to find solutions to his money problems himself?

Now that we've identified the four most common relapse triggers, the second step in insuring your family against an A.C.E.S. relapse is learning to do an exercise called "*Playing the Tape Through*."

"Playing the Tape Through" is an expression that was inspired by video and audio tape (if you were born before 1990, you surely know about these ancient materials). Before the dawn of the digital world, recordings were made using video and audio tape and it took time to rewind or fast forward the tapes to get to a desired place in each recording. Videotape, in particular, was a phenomenal invention that made entertainment convenient to say the least. The benefit of videotaped movies, for example, was that people could watch a portion of a film, stop it, and then come back to watch the rest at a convenient time. Fast forwarding or rewinding videotape in order to skip or review particular scenes made it easy to avoid unpleasant scenes or to repeat/review others. If the movie looked as though it was progressing towards a lousy ending (e.g. sad, disappointing or disturbing), one could simply eject the videotape and skip the ending entirely. But naturally, one would have to *"Play the tape through"* if he was interested in knowing how the movie ends.

A.C.E.S. parents who practice the *"Playing the Tape Through"* exercise find it to be an excellent tool in preventing an A.C.E.S. relapse. If you find yourself considering whether to allow your adult-child to move back in with you for a reason other than a **legitimate** emergency, first stop and *play the tape all the way through*, skipping nothing. In order to make the right decision, you must consider how that decision is *likely* to play out. That is, you must take a good honest look at the likelihood of negative consequences and that can only be done via historical review.

Look at the history of your relationship with your adult-child. Have you made impulsive decisions based on emotionality that led to negative consequences (such as damaging your own credit when you co-signed for him on a car loan)? What were the circumstances? What was your *true* motivation in making such decisions? Access the rational side of your brain and determine whether decisions you made on behalf of your adult-child were based on reality-based data or dysfunctional emotionality. See where you abandoned logic in favor of avoiding even mild emotional discomfort. Go ahead and *play the tape through* to the bitter end. Honestly, did your decisions facilitate resourcefulness and maturity? Or did they perpetuate unhealthy dependency? How did the story end?

The following is an example of someone who should have *played the tape through* but did not.

A recovering alcoholic, Fred, who had been sober for six months started to feel very bored living a sober life. He remembered all the fun he had when he used to drink freely but deliberately did not review the bad times his alcohol consumption brought about. So Fred decided to drink again. Unwilling to dwell on the mistakes he'd made when drinking, he simply promised himself that, this time, he would not get carried away.

The evening Fred started drinking again, he had two or three drinks and was having a wonderful time. He was enjoying himself with friends he hadn't seen for months. They talked about all the good times they had had before he stopped coming around. Fred was the life of the party and began wondering why he had ever decided to give up drinking in the first place.

As the evening progressed, Fred continued to drink and eventually became thoroughly intoxicated. He lost track of how much alcohol he had consumed. Eventually, Fred blacked out. He woke up on the lawn of a neighbor with no recollection of how he'd gotten there. He found his car up the block a bit and saw that it was wrapped around his neighbor's tree. He became conscious of a pain in his head and reached up to his forehead to find a giant bloody gash.

Fred had to wake up his wife so she could take him to the hospital's emergency room.

Fred was humiliated and his family was disgusted with him. He felt tremendous remorse for his decision to drink again and wondered why he had gotten himself into such a mess: AGAIN!

The alcoholic in the above vignette decided to drink again largely because he failed to *play the tape through*. He thought only of the good times he had when he was drinking. He thought nothing of the horrendous consequences he'd suffered when overdrinking in the past. He had a history with alcohol that included mostly *negative* consequences but he chose not to thoroughly review the negative consequences when he made his decision to drink again. He brushed those thoughts away by making a quick mental promise not to over-do it. A history lesson is, in part, about memorizing facts. A value-rich part of knowing history is that it can help us avoid making the same mistakes that we made in the past under similar circumstances. *Playing the tape through* is an exercise in making use of relevant history.

Specifically, in regards to a situation where your adult-child asks to move home, say "No." Can you find any historical data that would indicate letting him move back in will work out well? I doubt it.

By the way, in case you have not already discerned this by yourself, your adult-child is *likely* to run into trouble when he is on his own for the first time. He may have financial difficulties or logistical problems with roommates and whatnot. That's normal. And in families without A.C.E.S., it would be normal for parents to help their young adult-child out a bit. But this book is about adult-children who have been adults for quite some time. It is about adult-children who feel ***entitled*** to be cared for, bailed out, rescued, and BABIED by their parents. And it is about parents who are dysfunctionally compelled to enable infantile behavior on the part of their adult-children in order to avoid their own emotional problems.

Let me be blunt: But for a DIRE emergency, DO NOT ALLOW YOUR ADULT-CHILD TO MOVE BACK HOME ONCE HE HAS BEEN LAUNCHED. I will define *emergency* later (*see the end of this chapter*). But for now understand that to allow him to move home when he is merely struggling will only succeed in undermining his confidence. He needs to recognize that he can independently resolve the problems that are triggering his desire to return to YOUR home. Additionally, if you place yourselves in a position to fall into old dysfunctional patterns, you probably will. In other words, if you do not *play the tape through* and envision what it would be like to have your adult-child living with you again, you could reignite your family's compulsion to triangulate. You could find yourselves in an A.C.E.S. relapse.

Think back to the times when you have invited your adult-child into the private matters of your marital relationship. Reflect on how having close proximity to your adult-child made it that much easier to triangulate her. She was someone to talk to who knew your spouse's faults. Your adult-child was witness to many of your marital arguments over the years. You may feel that she understands and supports you more than anyone else ever could. But honestly recollect what triangulation ultimately did to your marriage. Think of how it stunted your adult-child's emotional development and handicapped her when it came to taking personal responsibility for her own life. Knowing all you know now, why would you put yourselves at risk for triangulation and a potential A.C.E.S. relapse by (unnecessarily) letting her move home again?

Here is an example of how triangulation might re-present itself if you were to allow your adult-child to move back into your home:

1. You and your spouse have an argument and you decide to vent about it to your adult-child.

2. You and your adult-child, who may have a similar point of view, form an unspoken alliance against your spouse based on your mutual perspective on the particular issue.

3. Your adult-child, feeling guilty for taking sides, may feel obligated to act as a mediator between you and your spouse. She might be used as a medium for marital communication.

4. Your adult-child's presence in your home enables you and your spouse to avoid direct communication and inhibits marital intimacy. Ordinary conflicts between you and your spouse might go ignored and unresolved because you don't want to argue in front of your adult-child (who is always around).

5. Marital tension may increase due to the frequency of unresolved conflicts. Your marital system may begin to atrophy if it is forced to rely on a third party (your adult-child) to diffuse tension in the relationship.

6. An emotional dependency upon your adult-child to remain at home may persuade you not to encourage her to re-launch herself into the world of personal responsibility.

7. Your adult-child may feel a renewed sense of obligation to remain at home to keep your marriage from splitting up.

8. A.C.E.S. relapse.

To the Adult-Child

Most of this book is directed to the marital-unit in your family. You are not the cause of A.C.E.S. but you are its most visible *symptom*. Your sense of entitlement may have been caused by problems in your parents' marriage but changing your attitude and faulty thinking regarding your belief that you should be given unearned privileges, goods, and services now becomes your responsibility to correct.

In terms of relapse prevention, I ask you to consider your future. Imagine yourself 10 years from now if you were still living at home with your parents. Envision yourself in that scenario. Be sure to think about your financial situation, the state of your career, and your marital status. In this scenario, do you have a sense of pride about the way you are living? Imagine yourself being accountable to, and financially dependent upon, your parents at the age of 35, 40, 45 or older. Consider whether enduring temporary homesickness is worth it if you can thereby avoid the alternative of resuming a very dysfunctional way of being in the world. Is your independence worth sacrificing just to avoid the short-term discomfort of living on your own?

To Marital-Units AND Adult-Children

While it may seem like second nature to pick up the phone and overexpose the details of your personal life to your adult-child / parents, try to resist doing so. Simply put, do not continue to rely on your adult-child / parents for basic emotional support.

As no one person is able to meet all the emotional needs of another, consider relying more on same sex friends who can provide the day-to-day emotional support you need. Same sex friends aren't likely to damage marital relationships or facilitate dysfunctional relationships between adult-children and their parents. Most importantly, same sex emotional support almost certainly will not facilitate an A.C.E.S. relapse. Good friends can add some much needed balance to lives that have been thrown out of balance by A.C.E.S.

Of course A.C.E.S. parents and their adult-children do not have to be strangers who shouldn't communicate at all. It is perfectly fine and appropriate for an adult-child to talk to his parents about what's going on in his life from time to time. He may fittingly seek out his parents when he needs the wisdom of their life experiences to help him make major decisions. However, droning on with his mother or father about the minutia of his daily life will only lead him back to reliance on them to meet his social and emotional needs. If an adult-child fails to enlarge his social support system, he will be compromising his family's ability to prevent an A.C.E.S. relapse.

It is important for A.C.E.S. adult-children to make an effort to educate themselves about how to set appropriate boundaries with their parents and other family members. Adult-children who became accustomed to sharing the details about their private lives with their parents must now learn and practice *personal containment*, a critical aspect of setting and enforcing emotional boundaries. Learning how to contain one's private thoughts, and keep from sharing the personal details about one's life with those who don't need to know such information, may help adult-children avoid the perpetuation of A.C.E.S. in the families they will likely create at some point in the future. Personal counseling can be very helpful when it comes to learning how to set firm and appropriate boundaries. Books about codependency can also guide you in how to set boundaries in loving and respectful ways.

Try not to forget how long it took your family to address and recover from A.C.E.S. Based on the history of your family, it may seem like a relapse is unavoidable. But that sort of defeatist thinking will only enable inappropriate behaviors. If you have been able to follow through on goals that were set throughout the A.C.E.S. recovery process, relapse may never become an issue. If you are able to maintain the boundaries and limits you agreed to when you decided to embark upon this process, a relapse is actually highly *unlikely*.

Emergency Circumstances

As promised, I have identified some emergency circumstances which might warrant a decision to allow your adult-child to move back into your home. *To be clear, an emergency circumstance is an urgent situation that has the potential to trigger a disaster if it is not directly circumvented through external means.*

The following is a list of situations that might qualify as legitimate emergencies.

1. If your adult-child becomes seriously ill and cannot adequately care for herself, you may want her in your home so you can care for her properly until she is well.
2. If there was a flood or fire in your adult-child's apartment and he has lost all his possessions and has nowhere to go in the short-term, you would compassionately welcome him back home for a period of time with the understanding that it is to be temporary living situation.
3. If your adult-child has been psychologically traumatized by an unforeseeable event, such as a crime, you may feel it best to allow him to move home for a short while so he can recover control of his nerves in a loving and supportive environment.
4. If your adult-child is being stalked by someone and needs protection until the maniac after your kid has been apprehended, go ahead and let her move in for a while.

Most of these sorts of circumstances probably won't happen, thank goodness. That's why we can refer to them as *emergency circumstances*. The following is a list of non-emergencies that may feel/seem like real emergencies.

1. Your adult-child wants to move home because he is fighting with his roommate.
2. He is having trouble making ends meet.
3. She is lonely.
4. He is bored.

5. He has some other problem that he can, and should, handle on his own.

If it has been determined that your adult-child is in the midst of an actual emergency situation, and you have decided to let her move back into your home temporarily, you can prevent the likelihood of an A.C.E.S. relapse by adhering to some specific guidelines.

1. A specific timeline should be set. Will your adult-child live with you for two weeks or two months? A discussion should be made about how long your adult-child expects to be living in your home.

2. Rent and other expenses should be required of your adult-child on a weekly basis, as if he or she was staying in a hotel. If he lost all his possessions as a result of his emergency, he will obviously need to accumulate some funds before he can move back out of your home. Therefore, you will have to subjectively determine how much of a contribution you should receive from your adult-child in exchange for room and board in your home. If your adult-child loses his source of income because of his emergency (e.g., having become too ill to work), you will likewise have to determine how he can compensate you for opening your home to him. Naturally, you will err on the side of compassion when it is appropriate but remember not to enable dependency. To that end, if his emergency has had no impact on his ability to generate income and he simply stops working once he is back home with you, claiming he doesn't have any money to pay you for room and board, he should be directed to a shelter for indigent gentleman. *(I know this sounds harsh or even implausible, but the point is that you have to be steadfast in your commitment to hold your adult-child responsible for his own welfare. Otherwise, you may be taking care of him forever).*

3. The adult-child should only unpack his toiletries and clothes into your home. Other belongings should remain boxed and

stored. The room he occupies while in your home should not be altered to accommodate a permanent resident. Your adult-child can sleep on a couch or a pull-out sofa if a guest bedroom is not available.

4. It should be discussed and made clear that these guidelines are being followed so as to *avoid* an A.C.E.S. relapse. It is not about heartlessness or lack of caring. As a matter of fact, it is the exact opposite.

Chapter 5 – Conclusion

After living a certain way for so long, the A.C.E.S. recovery program may seem like an overwhelming process to some families. It is true that A.C.E.S. recovery is quite demanding emotionally, psychologically, and interpersonally. To fully enact the strategies outlined in this book may be very difficult for a myriad of reasons, and to differing degrees, depending on the particulars of each family-unit.

While this book has shown that A.C.E.S. originally stems from dysfunctional marital-units, I want my readers to understand that it gains strength from other sources as well. I will identify these sources and expound upon them accordingly in the coming pages.

But firstly, I want to offer some comfort to those couples who feel a sense of failure because they weren't able to launch their adult-children into the world without assistance. Let me suggest that rather than regretting past mistakes, look forward to, and peacefully accept, whatever life has in store for you now. Fortunately, you were able to find this book which has given you practical guidelines that, when strictly applied, will allow your family to break free of A.C.E.S.' grip. But be aware that you will have a few things working against you in spite of your conscientious application of the A.C.E.S. recovery process. Those *things* (i.e., "other sources" as referenced above) are what I'd like to call to your attention in my conclusion.

1. Societal Influence

The reason this book was written to families, as opposed to society as a whole, is because problems like A.C.E.S. can only be cured at the family level. Simply put, A.C.E.S. is remedied through the diligent application of the guidelines contained in this book and can only be executed via A.C.E.S. family members.

However, it's important to bear in mind that society's ability to influence minds and attitudes is very powerful. It helps to form attitudes about everything from body image to organic foods to recycling to religion to fitness to sexuality to lifestyle choices and to everything in between. And of course it also influences our attitudes about personal responsibility and our feelings about entitlements. Make no mistake, societies have the capacity to nurture cultures of dependency or to cultivate personal responsibility. The risk of such powerful societal influence is that it has the potential to interfere with peoples' ability to identify their own personal motivators. It could also inhibit peoples' desire to initiate positive growth-oriented goals. A society of individuals that lack the motivation to achieve meaningful goals cannot be sustained. We must be moving forward or we stagnate and eventually lose ground.

When societies reflect the belief that adult-children cannot and should not be accountable for obtaining basic life-necessities via their own productive efforts, future generations are placed in jeopardy. We must resist the temptation to give that which is unearned to those capable of earning. And this must start at the family level. Your ability to eradicate A.C.E.S in your family proves that paths leading to permanent dependency and feelings of entitlement can be repaved in the direction of independence and personal responsibility. Just think: *If something can be realized at the family level, it can probably be realized at the community level and beyond.*

2. Childhood Education

A sense of entitlement is achieved incrementally, over time. With the best of intentions, elementary schools can foster the sense of entitlement in very young children, many of whom grow into A.C.E.S. adult-children. For example, many public school systems have initiated programs to "boost self-esteem" in children. But their approaches, well-intentioned though they may be, actually do just the opposite.

For instance, my young daughter goes to a school that has a Student of the Month award. When my daughter brought home a notice saying that she had been selected as the Student of the Month, my husband and I were very proud! We went to the awards ceremony at her school to see her receive her award only to discover that she was one of *five* students in her class of 25 children that won the award that month. As a matter of fact, five students were selected from *each* of the 15 classes in the school who each won the Student of the Month award. We later learned that **every student** in the school would win the award at some point during the year. "Winning" that award did not make my daughter feel special. The award was meaningless to her because it was so diluted. Her self-esteem was actually compromised by the whole thing because she knew she did nothing to earn the award.

I don't need to explain the folly in the idea behind the Student of the Month award but I will. Each student only needs to wait his turn to be Student of the Month. He doesn't have to earn it. He is entitled to "win" the award just for breathing in and out.

You know firsthand that A.C.E.S. adult-children feel entitled to be given food, shelter, transportation, medical care, companionship, and miscellaneous without earning any of those things. As you've come to understand, their collective sense of entitlement was born at home but was probably reinforced at school.

My daughter's school also has an annual talent show. But a winner is never selected. The theory is that no one should be made to feel inadequate for not being the best. What is wrong with being the best? A more important question is what is wrong with allowing our kids to learn how to tolerate disappointment? What's wrong with them being motivated by the *chance* to be recognized as the winner? What's wrong with failing at something if our children get the opportunity to develop tenacity out of the experience? Our kids won't suffer the loss of self-esteem because they lost a contest, they will gain self-esteem by having the courage to compete for the win!

Offering unearned rewards leads only to mediocrity, complacency and lack of purpose. Receiving unearned awards renders the awards meaningless to the recipients.

3. Other Families with A.C.E.S.

Parents know how hard it is to refuse their children something that their friends all seem to have.

My daughter is 11. She wants a smart phone. She doesn't need a smart phone. I don't want her distracted by a smart phone. She's not getting a smart phone, at least not for now. But many of her friends have smart phones. So my daughter wants one and thinks she *should* have one. It's my job to deconstruct that faulty belief or I might wind up with a case of A.C.E.S. down the line!

This same daughter has to do chores to earn spending money. Most often, she does chores because she is told to do them. When she receives money for doing a good job, it's a pleasant surprise to her. She doesn't expect to be paid for helping to maintain our household. She understands that part of belonging to a family means that we all have to do our share of the work. But her friends *tell* their parents they *need* money and their parents give it to them whether they earn it or not. When mothers and fathers give their children money for the asking, their children believe they are *entitled* to it. And, as A.C.E.S. parents know, this belief does not magically die off when their children become adults.

A.C.E.S. adult-children seem to find and befriend other A.C.E.S. adult-children. Your adult-child may have friends whose families are still entrenched in A.C.E.S. If that is the case, you are sure to experience a lot of "But Megan's parents pay for her cell phone" and "Bob's dad gave him a car" or "Andy's mom says he can live with her as long as he wants."

To be sure, chronic exposure to the shenanigans of other (unrecovered) A.C.E.S. families will not make your recovery process any easier. So be aware of their presence in your adult-child's life and do your best to contrast their unhealthy A.C.E.S. tendencies with your adult-child's new and improved attitudes and behaviors.

In closing, let me give you some good news. You are now in a position to contribute to the renaissance of personal responsibility, self-reliance, and *genuine* self-esteem among adult-children by spreading the word about the A.C.E.S recovery process. So many families need to know that there is a way out of this destructive syndrome and your experience and success in arresting A.C.E.S. in your own family may inspire other families to recover as well. Do not be shy about sharing this book with friends and extended family that may be in the same boat as your family was prior to A.C.E.S.

recovery. Friends and family are likely to need your support as they struggle through the different phases of A.C.E.S. recovery.

As previously stated, once you complete the A.C.E.S. recovery program, you will be in a very impactful position to be helpful to other families because they will be inspired by your family's recovery. Your family will display the wonderful fruits of A.C.E.S. recovery. Your marriage will thrive as intimacy is established and reinforced over time. And your adult-child will assume his rightful place in society as a fully-functioning adult.

Made in the USA
Las Vegas, NV
19 June 2021